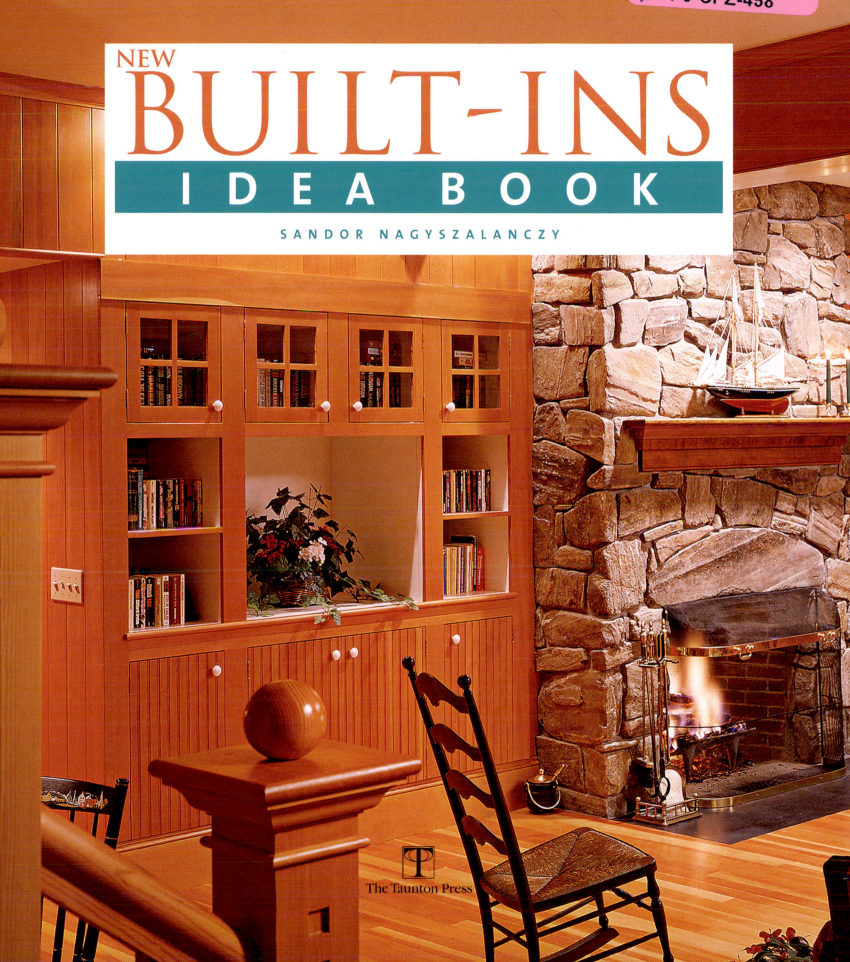

NEW
BUILT-INS
IDEA BOOK

SANDOR NAGYSZALANCZY

The Taunton Press

The Taunton Press, Inc., 63 South Main Street, PO Box 5506, Newtown, CT 06470-5506
e-mail: tp@taunton.com

EDITOR: Stefanie Ramp

JACKET/COVER DESIGN: Jeannet Leendertse

INTERIOR DESIGN: Lori Wendin

LAYOUT: Cathy Cassidy

FRONT COVER PHOTOGRAPHERS: Top row: (left and far right) © 2004 Carolyn L. Bates–carolynbates.com; (second and third from left) © Phillip Ennis Photography. Middle row: (first, second, and third from left) © Phillip Ennis Photography; (far right) © Mark Samu. Bottom row: (left to right) © Brian Vanden Brink, Photographer 2004; © Phillip Ennis Photography; © Mark Samu; © www.davidduncanlivingston.com
BACK COVER PHOTOGRAPHERS: Top: © Phillip Ennis Photography. Bottom row: (left to right) © Robert Perron, Photographer; © 2004 Carolyn L. Bates–carolynbates.com; © Ken Gutmaker

Library of Congress Cataloging-in-Publication Data
Nagyszalanczy, Sandor.
  New built-ins idea book / Sandor Nagyszalanczy.
     p. cm.
  ISBN-13: 978-1-56158-673-8
  ISBN-10: 1-56158-673-0
  1. Built-in furniture--Design and construction. 2. Cabinetwork. 3. Storage in the home. I. Title.

TT197.5.B8N34 2004
684.1'6--dc22
                                    2004018190
Printed in the United States of America
15 14 13

The following manufacturers/names appearing in *New Built-Ins Idea Book* are trademarks: Corian®, Formica®

Contents

Introduction

In the early part of the last century, only the affluent could afford to have finely constructed built-in furnishings added to their homes. A grand home, like the Greene & Greene-designed Gamble House in Pasadena, California, was graced with custom-made stairways, fireplaces, even light fixtures, and had extensive built-in furniture and cabinetry in every room.

Fortunately, in recent decades built-ins have become part of the contemporary American concept of what makes up the interior of a home—whether it's a mansion or a starter model. The right built-ins afford a home many important qualities, including utility, comfort, and style.

Cabinets and shelves have the utilitarian function of storing our clothing or organizing our books. Window seats and benches add comfort to our homes by

creating cozy places to relax or congregate. Well-designed built-ins and the trim, paneling, and other components that enhance their installation can add warmth, color, and tons of style to any room of the house, transforming spaces from drab to delightful. Besides making an interior more pleasurable to live in, built-ins also can add to the value of your home—yet another compelling reason to consider them.

The rising popularity of the DIY (do-it-yourself) movement and the spread of home centers and internet web sites has greatly helped to make the possibility of creating and installing your own built-ins a reality. There's a seemingly endless selection of products—everything from knock-down cabinetry to shelf and closet organizer systems to counter and work surface materials. There are also countless options for bathroom, kitchen, and lighting fixtures, and hardware for doors, drawers, racks, shelves, and more.

But before you begin making the multitude of decisions your remodeling or home upgrade job will entail, you must begin with ideas. That's where this book comes in. The following 10 chapters are organized by rooms: passages (hallways, entryways, and staircases), kitchens, bathrooms, living areas, entertainment areas, bedrooms, kids' rooms, work spaces, and utility areas. There's also a first chapter that's intended to help you better plan your built-ins, as well as effectively integrate them with the room's paneling, doors and windows, and trim.

Throughout these pages, you'll find lots of impressive examples of built-ins for every room in the house. The photos were taken in well-designed homes and apartments all over America, and range in style from country rustic to traditional colonial to casual contemporary to stark modern. Just leafing through the book, you're sure to glean lots of ideas about design, layout, and materials that will help you create your own vision, or make it easier for you to work with an interior designer, contractor, and/or builder on your project.

Whether you find a design that is exactly what you're looking for or you simply develop a better sense of the wide range of looks and configurations possible with built-ins, this book will be both helpful and inspirational.

Planning Built-Ins

IT'S CLEARLY UNWISE TO REMODEL A ROOM by adding a cabinet here and a little trim there, because you'll end up with a look that's random and thrown together rather than a cohesive design. By laying out a careful plan for built-ins, you'll achieve visual harmony as well as create elements that function efficiently and in accordance with your needs.

There are many points to consider before you start building. The style of the new built-ins (and trim) should synchronize with adjacent rooms and spaces. Placement of new built-ins should be planned carefully to ensure they don't interfere with traffic flow through the room or block light or a view through windows (this is especially important with large units that double as room dividers). Precise measurements should be taken to make sure cabinet drawers and doors have enough space to open without hitting walls or neighboring cabinetry (corner cabinets are especially prone to this). Also think about whether there are features that would enhance the built-in's purpose, for example, lighting or a small sink in a bar cabinet. Finally, make sure your built-ins are capable of accommodating future changes—bookshelves should be big enough to hold new acquisitions, for instance.

While it may seem overwhelming, a systematic exploration of these points will save you an incredible amount of time, money, and headache in the long run, and ensure that your investment in built-ins was a worthwhile one.

◄ **WELL-DESIGNED BUILT-IN CABINETRY** can serve as the centerpiece of a room. This U-shaped island not only provides lots of workspace for the kitchen, but it also allows the hosts to entertain and interact with guests while they're cooking.

CHOOSING THE COMPONENTS

Once you've arrived at a built-in design that's right for the space you're decorating or remodeling, you're ready to choose materials, hardware and fixtures, and lighting. Although the cabinetry and other built-ins in most homes have traditionally been constructed from wood, there is a plethora of other materials to work with. These include both natural materials, such as marble, granite, and bamboo, and man-made materials, such as stainless steel, plastic laminates (e.g. Formica®), and solid-surface materials (e.g. Corian®).

While choosing a built-in's material is the first and most important step, selecting the proper hardware, fixtures, and lighting for the unit will enhance both its form and function. These seemingly little details can have a big impact on a built-in's (and room's) style, whether it be traditional, modern, or eclectic. They can also ensure that a built-in lives up to the vision you had in mind; for instance, without recessed lighting, the cabinet of glass shelves you designed to hold your prized collection of antique china could offer only a lackluster performance.

Materials

Choosing the right material can have a profound effect on both the look and the functionality of a room. For example, installing a stainless-steel backsplash and range hood in a kitchen with plastic-laminate-covered cabinets creates a very clean look that's seminal to a contemporary-style kitchen. In contrast, choosing natural bamboo for a

tansu-style built-in dresser and headboard along with a tatami-mat floor treatment would be excellent choices for a room with a distinctly Asian flavor.

Altering just one material of a built-in can dramatically change the overall look of a room: Imagine changing the countertop of a built-in bar from natural wood to colored concrete or perhaps to a glitzy plastic laminate with a metallic-finish; in each case, the look of the entire bar is transformed from traditional to hip and modern.

Hardware and Fixtures

Once the big decision concerning primary material is made, it's time to select hardware and fixtures that will accompany and enhance your built-ins. From bathrooms to kitchens to bars, your choice of fixtures and other hardware should match both the style and the coloration of the room.

Choices for bathroom sinks and tubs are particularly daunting, as some of the more complex units, such as whirlpool tubs with powered water jets, often require special built-in enclosures to accommodate wiring and plumbing. Faucets also come in a wide array of styles and finishes (chrome, gold, antique brass, brushed stainless, and many others), with other hardware (towel bars, soap holders, and hooks, for instance) finished to match.

For the hardworking built-ins found in kitchens and family rooms, there's a great variety of nuts-and-bolts hardware to enhance the functionality of your cabinets and media centers, including special bins for trash and recycling, lazy Susans that make corner cabinets more functional, and

▲ MATERIALS, COLORS, AND TEXTURES are all valuable elements at your control when decorating—or redecorating—a space. This log-cabin-like kitchen features a dark wood for its cabinetry and tile counters, creating an appealing contrast with the light wood used in most of the room.

◄ THE OPEN DESIGN OF THESE MODERN-COUNTRY CABINETS allows for display as well as ultimate accessibility. The cabinet knobs were painted white and distressed, adding a hardware detail that reinforces the kitchen's style.

▲ THIS ELEGANT, ARCHED-ALCOVE BUILT-IN features lower cabinets for discreet storage and shelves above. The recessed light in the apex of the arch illuminates the glass shelf below, creating a simple but dramatic display space.

pullout shelf units for TVs and other electronics. The decorative hardware, such as cabinet and drawer pulls, also helps create a cohesive, aesthetically pleasing style.

Lighting

Lighting is another important consideration, especially with extensive built-ins such as wall units, large headboards, and entertainment centers. Installing lights and lighting controls directly into such units has an obvious functional value, as it provides readily accessible illumination when you're trying to find something in a cabinet, read in bed, or operate the DVD or stereo.

But accent lighting in smaller units also should be considered, for it can help create ambiance or set the mood of a room. For example, incorporating track lights or recessed "can" lighting into the top of a shelf unit can spotlight sculptures or art objects for a dramatic effect.

INTEGRATING BUILT-INS

Once you've chosen the style and design of built-in furnishings and planned their placement, it's time to look carefully at how these new pieces will be integrated into the room they'll be installed in. If you've chosen to build with wood, pay close attention to the type of finish you use. You're first thought may be to match existing finishes or colors, but you may find that you can create a truly unique and personal statement by contrasting with them.

▲ **COVERED, PAINTED BEAMS** against this narrow-slat, natural-wood ceiling help create a more integrated look with the room's white window frames and built-in bed and cabinetry. The wood on the ceiling and floor add warmth that helps keep the room from feeling too bland or sterile.

▲ **AN EFFECTIVE WAY TO INCORPORATE BUILT-IN CABINETRY** with the rest of a room's furnishings is to employ repeating motifs or distinctive materials. Here, natural wood logs are used throughout this contemporary rustic interior—even for the legs of the dining table unit, which also houses several storage shelves.

▲ **MATCHING THE HEIGHT OF BUILT-IN CABINETRY**, particularly if it's large scale, with other features of a room helps create a seamless, unified look. These tall, narrow cases are in line with the trim above the French doors they flank, balancing them with the other architectural details in the room.

Also think about how new built-ins can be tied into the room with complementary moldings, wainscoting, and door and window trim. For instance, what crown and baseboard moldings will work best around kitchen cabinets? By carefully planning the entire look of your room before building, you're much more likely to end up with a room that's a pleasure to be in.

DO-IT-YOURSELF OR HIRE HELP?

If you have a creative streak, then designing and planning your built-ins can be a very enjoyable experience. But if the creative process isn't your cup of tea, you can still participate in the design process by gathering ideas from various sources: Clip photos from magazines and catalogs and earmark the pages of this book that have examples of pieces you like. Showing these to an interior designer or custom cabinetmaker is a great first step toward creating built-in furnishings you'll be pleased with.

◀ A USEFUL TECHNIQUE FOR ADDING BUILT-INS to space-challenged rooms is to "steal" a little space from an adjoining area. This relatively shallow cabinet penetrates marginally into the area behind the wall, so it doesn't rob one square inch from the small living room it services.

▲ A WELL-PLANNED INSTALLATION OF BUILT-INS not only improves the look and value of your house but the usefulness of certain spaces as well. The substantial, closet-like built-ins added to this large, open-ceiling room effectively provide amenities that make working in the space much easier.

▲ **INSPIRED THINKING AND GOOD PLANNING** can make the most of oddly-shaped spaces that might otherwise go to waste. These display shelves, which were built into the sloping sections of this attic room, are a good example of creative design. They'd also make a challenging but feasible project for a home craftsman.

The DIY Route

Once your plans and ideas are assembled, it's time to move on to the building stage. If you feel comfortable with the scale and complexity of a project, you may decide to build and install it yourself. If you're a home craftsman with the skills, time, and space to tackle a modest project, then going the do-it-yourself route can be very rewarding, as well as economical.

Most modern home centers and building supply stores (not to mention catalog and internet suppliers) stock cabinetry and hardware supplies that allow home craftsmen to create and install their own built-ins. This includes everything from basic shelf and closet organizing systems to knock-down cabinets that assemble quickly and easily into an entire kitchen's worth of cabinets.

Hiring a Professional

On the other hand, if the built-ins you envision are extensive and/or complex, then hiring a qualified builder may be your best choice. Many of the built-ins shown in this book are unique pieces designed to fit a particular space or fill a particular need—a multi-drawered cabinet made to hold a stamp collection, a desk with shelves and compartments sized to accommodate a computer system, a bunk bed alcove that creates a cozy sleeping space for a child. Such pieces can only be built from scratch starting with raw materials—solid woods, plywoods, veneer, stone, etc. Although it may be expensive, hiring a professional is the best way to end up with quality built-ins that are functional, attractive pieces you'll be proud to have in your home.

▲ AN EXTENSIVE BUILT-IN TREATMENT can make even a small room an effective multifunctional space. For example, this room provides a computer work area, as well as shelves for art and books, cabinetry for glassware, and a counter for eating. For a project of this size and complexity, it's best to hire a professional.

Passages

WHEN IT COMES TO TRAVEL, they say that getting there is half the fun. Why shouldn't that be true for your home as well? Hallways, stairways, doorways, and entryways are all parts of a house primarily used to get from one space to another, but with a little creative effort, they can become more useful, decorative spaces—or even destinations in their own right.

Installing bookcases, shelves, drawer banks, or cabinets in a passage area can add lots of storage space for books, CDs, photographs, sports equipment, and more. Better still, locating built-ins in transition spaces like hallways and stairwells creates storage without robbing floor area from space-challenged living quarters.

Built-in cabinetry and trim details can also serve to make a home's transition areas, such as entryways and doorways between rooms, more welcoming and attractive. For example, walnut or oak wainscoting and a bench seat in an entry hall greets visitors with the warm look of wood, as well as provides a place to park while removing a scarf and galoshes. Likewise, most homes have other passage areas—like stairway landings and dormer alcoves—where the addition of a built-in transforms an otherwise lackluster part of the house into a comfortable space worth spending time in.

◄ **WHILE THE LIVING ROOM OR DEN** might be the destination, doorways, hallways, and stairs are the passageways that help you get there. Imbuing these transitional spaces with the right elements of design, including materials, trim, and built-in cabinetry, helps make them more interesting and useful parts of the home.

Entryways & Doorways

WHEN MOST PEOPLE THINK OF THE ENTRYWAYS and doorways around their homes, they don't necessarily think of them as likely places for adding built-in furniture or cabinetry. But these portals between indoors and out, and between one part of the house and another, as in the case of doorways, are locations worthy of the same consideration given to other areas of the home. Entryways are a prime candidate for built-in treatments, such as coat cabinets, racks, parcel shelves, or bench seats where guests and family members can change and store their indoor and outdoor gear. And cabinetry, open shelving, or wainscoting and trim added around a doorway can visually frame the space that lies beyond. These types of built-ins provide a relatively easy way of transforming an otherwise blah door opening between rooms into something that not only improves interior appearance but may also offer storage and/or display space.

▲ REPEATING A SIMPLE MOTIF, the curved rail atop this arched doorway echoes the shape of the nook to the left of it, creating visual flow. This entryway built-in includes two small closets, a coat rack, and a bench seat with drawer, which provides a welcoming spot when coming in from the cold.

▲ THIS PAIR OF BUILT-IN HUTCHES, with glass-enclosed shelves above and drawers below, straddles the doorway between dining room and den. Painting the cabinets white helps integrate them with the trim surrounding the doorway.

▲ SURROUNDING THIS DOORWAY WITH
BUILT-IN SHELVES eases the transition
from room to hallway, while providing
lots of space to display objects of
interest. The top of this built-in is
wide enough for larger items, such as
these baskets.

Using a Doorway to Frame a Space

ANY DOORWAY OR ENTRYWAY creates a frame around the space that lies beyond it. Door casings and trim traditionally serve to mask the seam between a door-frame and the surrounding wall, but this is basic and boring. A more interesting approach is to use shapely moldings and other architectural details that echo the paneling or trim in adjacent rooms. Better still, adding soffits and built-in cabinets or shelves around a doorway can create a truly unique and custom look while providing display and storage space as well.

Hallways

HOW MANY TIMES HAVE YOU WALKED DOWN A WIDE HALLWAY in your home and thought, "I should do something with that wasted floor space?" Once again, built-ins can come to the rescue, providing shelves or enclosable cabinetry for display and storage of all kinds of things. For example, consider fitting a set of low (30-in.- to 42-in.-tall) open-front cabinets along one side of a long hallway that connects several rooms. The cabinet's shelves can hold photo albums, books, magazines, and such, while the top of the cabinet creates a narrow counter that's great for showing off pottery or baskets, even houseplants. If your hallway is narrower, you can mount racks or slim shelves higher up on the wall where they won't be brushed against when someone walks by. In a bedroom hallway recess with nearby closets, installing a narrow bench with a lift-up seat (for shoe storage) can transform the space into a dressing area.

◄ A PADDED BENCH STEALS LITTLE SPACE from this entry hall but provides a place to sit while changing shoes or waiting for a ride. The bench, finished to match the door and surrounding trim, has an angled backrest that echoes the wainscoting in the kitchen.

► A HALLWAY NEED NOT BE A NARROW PASSAGE destined only for foot traffic. The addition of built-in shelving or cabinetry can transform any hall into a functional space with a character all its own. This example provides storage for books and display space for art.

▲ THE NATURAL WOOD FRAME-AND-PANEL TREATMENT in this hallway not only adds elegance to an otherwise plain space but also lends functional continuity. Both the closet doors and cabinet doors below the attractive alcove blend seamlessly with the hall's paneling.

▼ ▶ **TO BREAK UP THE LONG HALL THAT CONNECTS MANY ROOMS,** this home's designer decided to add several nooks along its length. One of the niches contains a built-in cabinet with a granite top. Another features a window seat and pillows.

Using a Hallway as a Transition

A WELL-DESIGNED HALLWAY can provide a graceful transition between one room in your home and another. For example, say you have a study with dark paneling that's down the hall from a brightly painted children's playroom. By painting or staining the trim in the hallway and the casing around its doorways a neutral color, you can ease the jump between the dark paneling of the study and the colorful walls of the playroom.

▲ COMPROMISED BY A SLOPING ROOF, the ceiling of this second-floor hallway angles down to a short wall that would be next to useless without the bank of built-ins. Not only do they add architectural interest, but they also provide storage that makes great use of otherwise wasted space.

▲ **A WIDE HALLWAY BETWEEN DINING ROOM AND KITCHEN** is transformed into a small pantry with the addition of built-in cabinetry. The floor-to-ceiling unit at left provides abundant dish and utensil storage, while the lower cabinet at right affords useful counter space.

► IN MOST HOMES, storage space is where you can find it. These linen cabinets were built into the wall of a hallway that connects several upstairs bedrooms, providing centralized storage without reducing floor space in any of the rooms.

◄ WITHOUT THE CURVED CABINETS and wainscoting, the look of this oddly-shaped passage would seem strange indeed. For a harmonious look, the built-in cabinetry at left was made the same height as the wainscoting below the glass-block window.

Stairways

DUE TO ITS ANGLED CONSTRUCTION, a stairway creates oddly-shaped spaces above and below it. Making good use of these spaces not only serves to better integrate a stairway into a home's overall décor, but makes it more functional and visually appealing as well. For example, adding a bank of drawers, pullouts, or cubbies in the triangular space left under a basic flight of stairs transforms wasted space into useful storage. Fitting the wall surfaces next to a stairway with shelves or nooks converts an otherwise ordinary wall into a mini-library or a gallery to show off collectibles. Not to be overlooked, the landings at the top of stairways are another ripe territory for adding built-ins, such as display shelves, love seats, or linen drawers.

▲ **A BENCH SEAT AND PILLOWS** transform this stairway landing into a cozy nook that's a comfortable space for reading, talking, or sipping wine. The white frame-and-panel seat, paneling, columns, and railings match the stairway's look and construction, visually fusing the staircase and built-in.

▲ **ALTHOUGH THEY REDUCE THE WIDTH OF THE STAIRS,** the addition of shelves and cubbies in this stairwell create useful storage and display space. The shelf's vertical supports also frame in a small window that's part way up the stairs for added visual interest.

◄ HALF-ROUND COLUMNS, ceiling treatments, and stair-tread trim help to unify this bookcase with an adjacent window and the curved stairway next to it. Extending the first three steps of the stairs to the bookcase helps make the stairs seem less narrow, while making the stairway and bookcase feel like part of one fluid unit.

▲ THREE BANKS OF DRAWERS and a triangular display nook add utility and style to the wasted space beneath this stairway. The contemporary look of these painted built-ins has origins in traditional Japanese tansu home furnishings.

▼ CONSISTENT TRIM AND FINISH TREAT-MENTS help meld a stairway with the floors and landings where the stairway starts and stops. For dramatic contrast, the handrail was designed to match the color of the floor, while the rest of the stairway, walls, and built-ins were painted white.

▲ THE CLEAR-FINISHED, NATURAL WOOD RAILINGS, posts, and balusters on this stairway work harmoniously with the stair treads and strip flooring. Low bookshelves make good use of the sloped-ceiling landing and help create a reading nook.

◄ THE STYLE OF A STAIRWAY should always match the space it's in. Painted metal posts strung with taut cables create a contemporary look that's supported by the use of bold color on the baseboards, window trim, and built-in drawer bank.

▲ RAILINGS AREN'T JUST FOR STAIRWAYS. The same natural-wood handrail and painted balusters used for the stairs were also employed to surround the mezzanine level of this home, creating a very light and airy feeling with abundant built-in book storage.

Kitchens and Dining Areas

F EW ROOMS ARE AS FREQUENTLY REMODELED as the kitchen. It's the room many of us spend much of our time in, and so it's a focal point of most homes, both visually and functionally.

Besides enhancing décor, a kitchen's built-ins, from cabinetry to islands, have many important duties to perform like providing storage and counter space and housing appliances. But built-ins also can serve other roles in the kitchen and dining area, such as displaying prized porcelain dishes, providing tables at which to sit and eat, creating racks to keep wine and spirits and pantries to store canned goods and bulk foods.

Built-in embellishments, such as ceiling treatments, trim, and wainscoting, are just as important for visual and functional harmony. For example, a soffit visually spans the gap between upper cabinets and the ceiling while also containing lighting for sinks and counter areas. Wainscoting serves to tie together sections of cabinetry as well as to protect lower walls from chair dings.

Whether you plan to tackle a full-on kitchen remodel—or just add a few new cabinets— the challenge is to synchronize your wishes and needs, selecting the right built-ins, trim, and hardware to make the room work. The ideas and examples shown in this chapter should help you get started toward realizing your dream kitchen.

◀ KITCHEN CABINETRY CAN BE MADE TO SUIT ANY SPACE—wide or narrow, cramped or expansive—and provide all the counter space, appliance housings, and storage that's needed for everything from foodstuffs to utensils to pots and pans. These cabinets were built with European-style construction and full-overlay doors for a clean, contemporary look.

Cabinetry

First and foremost, built-in kitchen cabinetry must be functional and provide storage for everything from cereal boxes to appliances, while also allowing for adequate counter space. But kitchen cabinets also should look good and harmonize with the overall style of your kitchen and the rest of your home's interior.

There are three kinds of basic built-in kitchen cabinets: lower, upper, and pantry. Lower cabinets are wide and deep and provide housing for big appliances, like ovens and dishwashers, as well as storage for heavy pots and pans, mixing bowls, and other large equipment; they may also contain drawers and pullouts for utensils and supplies. They are topped with counters, which provide work surfaces as well as places to mount sinks and set small appliances and other apparatus. Upper cabinets typically are shallower and have shelves that hold dishes and glassware. Pantry cabinets are tall, deep units that can run floor to ceiling and hold all manner of canned, bagged, or boxed foods, as well as sundry other kitchen provisions.

▲ THIS LARGE, PAINTED CABINET actually houses a refrigerator, keeping its modern look from clashing with this early-style country kitchen. The pair of doors opens out (the drawer fronts are false), with a cubby on top providing a small shelf for baskets.

◄ A WELL-PLANNED KITCHEN LAYOUT includes cabinets that accommodate all the needs of the modern kitchen: provide counter space for food preparation and cooking; house plumbing and appliances; store dishes and utensils; and even keep cookbooks organized yet handy.

▲ THE CLEAN DESIGN OF THESE BLONDE-WOOD CABINETS goes
well with the sleek look of the stainless steel appliances.
The full-overlay-style doors and drawer fronts are mounted
to cabinets that lack face frames, a construction style that
allows for larger drawers and yields easy access to cabinet
interiors.

◄ BUILT IN BETWEEN UPPER CABINETS
AND THE COUNTERTOP, an appliance
garage reduces clutter and keeps
toaster ovens, blenders, and canisters
clean but easily accessed. These cabinets feature a garage with framed
glass doors that open upwards and
slide back into the case.

► **THE MULTIPLE PANELS** in each of these frame-and-panel doors give the surface of the otherwise unadorned, white-painted cabinets some appealing texture. Wood counters, ordinary drawer pulls, and turn-knob latches keep the look clean and simple.

Kitchen Cabinetry Standards

THE MOST PRACTICAL APPROACH when designing a new or remodeled kitchen is to plan the layout around the standard dimensions for kitchen cabinetry. Standard heights and depths are typically the ones used by makers of commercial kitchen cabinets.

Even if you plan to install custom cabinets, you'll still want to adhere to most of these dimensions because most kitchen hardware, sinks, and appliances are designed to fit into cabinets with these sizes. Hence, if you decide to build lower cabinets that are shorter than the standard 34½ in., for example, you'll likely discover that a standard dishwasher won't fit.

Another important consideration is the length of counters in your kitchen's clean up/food preparation area, the cooking area, and the area near the refrigerator. The cleanup/food prep area is usually located around the sink and should have at least 18 in. of counter length on one side and 24 in. on the other. For example, if you have a 30-in.-wide sink, you'll want the sink counter to be just over 5 ft. long. The counter around the stove or range top should have the same arrangement as the sink counter. You should also plan to include a counter area that's at least 24 in. long next to or near the refrigerator for unloading bags of groceries and related tasks.

▲ **PAINTED CABINETS ADD COLOR AND CONTRAST** with the natural wood floors and paneling in this country-style home. Detailed touches maintain the rustic theme, such as a set of open shelves built around the corner log post and the log beam above the kitchen sink.

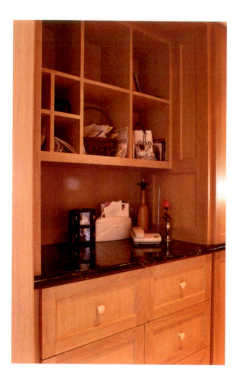

▲ **IN MANY HOUSEHOLDS,** the kitchen does double duty as a family activity center. In this kitchen, an open counter with cubbies above provides a place to keep a calendar, display family photos, organize bills and mail, make telephone calls, and take messages.

▲ **A SINGLE, CONTINUOUS ROW OF UPPER CABINETS** can make a narrow kitchen seem claustrophobic. Adding a plate rack between cabinets helps make the space feel more open, while still providing a place to keep treasured plates, which add a splash of decoration.

◄ **REMINISCENT OF CABINETS YOU'D FIND IN AN OLD APOTHE-CARY SHOP,** the tilt-out bins built into these lower kitchen cabinets hold split peas, pasta, and other dry goods. The clear panels make it easy to see the colorful contents of each bin.

▼ **POSITIONING THE KITCHEN SINK IN A CABINET** under a window or on a kitchen island makes it more comfortable to work at the sink. In cases where the sink must face a wall, as in this kitchen, raising the upper cabinets 30 in. or more above the countertop helps retain an open feeling.

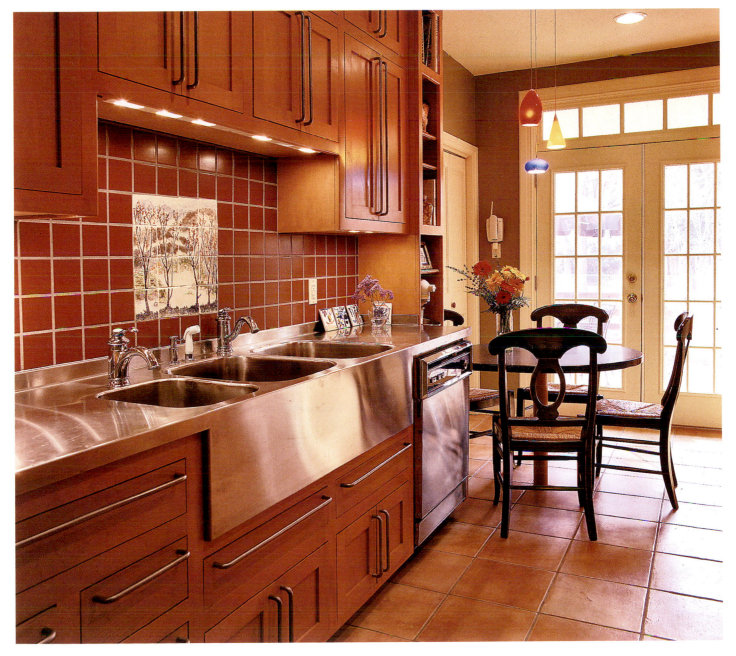

▲ **CANNED GOODS AND COOKWARE**
aren't the only things kitchen cabinets
are good for. These glass-doored upper
cabinets hold all of the glassware and
supplies for a bar, while the lowers
(ventilated to allow heat to escape)
house stereo components and speakers
for a kitchen serenade.

▲ **TIRED OF THE LOOK OF PLAIN OLD RECTILINEAR** kitchen cabinets? Throwing a few
curves into the design, like quarter-round open shelves at the end of the sink
counter and a curved rail highlighting the window and spanning the uppers, is an
easy, low-cost way to spice things up.

The Pantry

A LOVELY FEATURE found in the grand old houses of the Victorian era was the butler's pantry—an amply stocked supply room located near the kitchen. But just because you don't live in a huge Victorian home (or have a butler) doesn't mean you can't enjoy the convenience of a pantry.

A simple pantry need be nothing more than a tall cabinet with lots of shelves that can hold boxed foods, canned goods, spices and seasonings, kitchen supplies, and perhaps dishes and glassware. You can incorporate a pantry built-in directly into your kitchen cabinetry or add one in an adjacent room or hallway.

A well-designed pantry offers easy access to all of its contents. One approach is to make the cabinet very shallow, as seen in the photo below. A shallow pantry cabinet is terrific for small kitchens, since it can be added to a wall without taking up much floor space.

Another option is to make a deep cabinet and outfit it with relatively narrow shelves at the back and wire racks mounted to the door, as shown below. Pullout shelves and trays are another good way to make the contents of a deep pantry cabinet easy to access.

▲ THE TRADEOFF FOR MAKING PANTRY CABINETS DEEP and voluminous is that items buried at the back are hard to reach. Alternatively, the tall, shallow pantry cabinet shown here not only takes up little floor space but also makes every stored item easily accessible.

▲ TO MAKE THE MOST OF THE SPACE IN THIS DEEP PANTRY CABINET, the doors on the left side are fitted with wire racks that hold small canned goods and boxes. Racks on the left cabinet's bulkhead make the shallow shelves in back more accessible, as do the pullout racks in the right cabinet.

▼ WHEN IT COMES TO CABINETS FOR A RUSTIC KITCHEN, rough, irregular wood logs cut and made into the doors and drawer fronts of a built-in breakfront fit the bill nicely. A natural-edged countertop and accents made from smaller branches complete the effect.

▲ AMONG THE MANY VARIABLES TO CONSIDER when planning kitchen cabinets are the fixed dimensions of sinks and built-in appliances, and the size and location of windows and doorways. This small window seat makes a comfy place to sit, while taking advantage of the window and preventing gridlock between open doors in the two banks of cabinets.

▶ IN A MODERN KITCHEN, a refrigerator no longer has to look like a big, imposing appliance. The doors and drawers on most high-end built-in refrigerators are designed to accept overlay panels that can be made to suit any style of kitchen—even one that looks like a library.

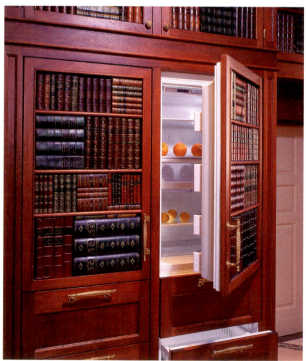

▲ **LIGHTING IS JUST AS IMPORTANT AS CABINET DESIGN** and layout in the overall planning of a kitchen. Modern overhead and under-cabinet lighting fixtures are compact and easy to mount into just about any kind of built-in, and they provide a kitchen with both illumination and ambiance.

Wine Racks

IDEALLY, YOU SHOULD KEEP YOUR FINEST WINES stored in the cellar—or at least in a cool closet or basement. But a wine rack will keep a few bottles handy at dinner time or when guests drop by. A good looking wooden wine rack that matches existing cabinetry and trim can be built into the dining area, perhaps as part of a sideboard or low, console-type cabinet. Alternatively, you can add a wood or commercially made metal rack to an existing lower or upper cabinet in the kitchen (see photo at right below). Just don't put the rack too close to a stove or other heat source (it's bad for the wine!).

An easy way to construct an attractive rack is by joining thin wood strips into a lattice-like configuration, as shown in the photo at left below. This type of rack has compartments that hold one bottle each, so any bottle can be removed without disturbing the others.

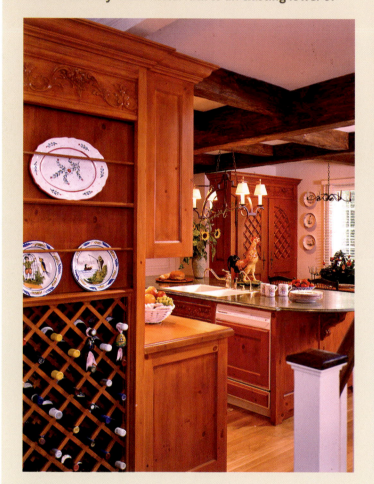

▲ **EVEN IF YOU HAVE THE LUXURY OF AN IN-HOUSE WINE CELLAR**, it's inconvenient to access it every time you need a bottle. A built-in wine rack, located either in or near the kitchen, is the ideal place to keep bottles on hand and ready to open when guests show up.

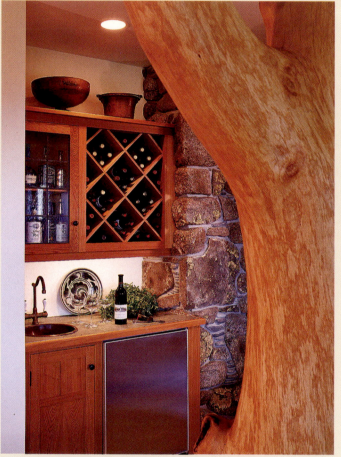

▲ **UPPER KITCHEN CABINETS ARE JUST THE RIGHT DEPTH** to store wine bottles, as done here in simple open bins made from the same wood as the cabinet doors and trim. This rack is conveniently located near a small refrigerator (for cooling white wines) and bar cabinet.

▲ MADE FROM NATURAL WOOD, this pantry area has lots of open storage for a variety of kitchen-related items, including dishes, cookbooks, and knick-knacks. The warmth and consistency of the wood help tie together the look of this eclectic space.

▲ GLASS PANELS USED IN WOOD CABINET DOORS are useful, as you can see what's in the cabinet before you open it, and decorative, as they create visual variety. For safety's sake, use tempered or safety glass for large doors that extend down near the floor, as shown here.

▲ **THE RIBBED GLASS** and the pattern of door muntins (cross members) retain this upper cabinet's open appearance, while muting the view of its contents—good if you're not obsessively neat. A continuous rail, located just at counter height, creates a visual separation between the top and bottom sections of the cabinet.

Hardware for the Kitchen

USUALLY MADE OF EITHER painted (or coated) metal wire or molded plastic, most kitchen hardware is designed to increase storage capacity, better organize a space, or make utensils and supplies more easily accessible.

Examples of kitchen hardware include pullout waste bins and recycling containers; holders for paper towels and bags; trays for brushes and cleaning supplies; organizers for silverware and cutlery; racks for spices, glassware, canned goods, and lots more. Fortunately, most hardware can be quickly and easily installed.

► TO MAINTAIN THE SPACIOUS FEELING OF THIS KITCHEN, a freestanding hutch, rather than a wall, is used to separate the kitchen from the adjacent room. Built to match the kitchen cabinets, the hutch has doors on both sides, making it useful in both rooms.

▼ UPPER KITCHEN CABINETS don't always need to have open counter space below. The arrangement here features a dish cupboard with a small drawer beneath—a very practical way to keep silverware or serving ware handy.

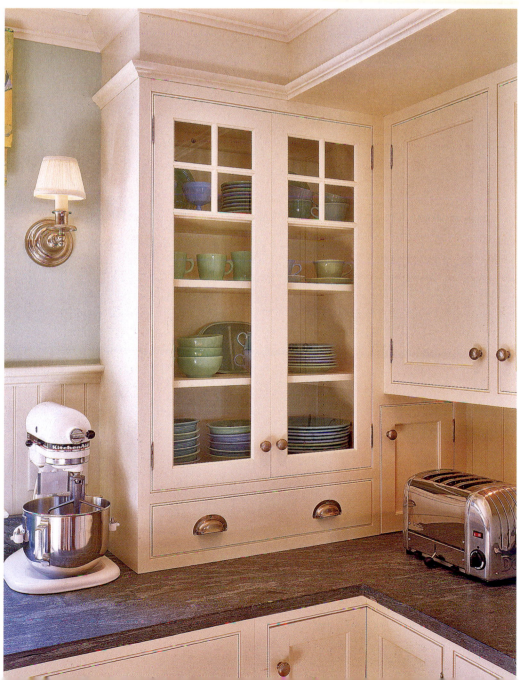

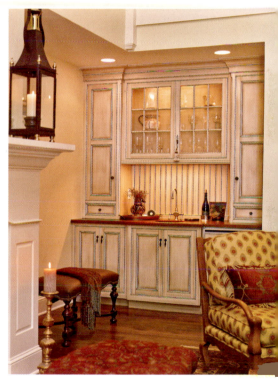

▲ BUILT-IN LIGHTING IS GREAT FOR ILLU-MINATING the usually decorative contents of a glass-doored cabinet, helping display them prominently, especially at night. The glass shelves in this cabinet allow the overhead light to pass through and reach objects on several levels.

▲ **MOST SERIOUS COOKS** want a big, commercial range like this one in their kitchen. Because of the heat they produce, big ranges and stoves require a non-flammable backsplash (here, stainless steel), lots of clearance for upper cabinets, and a large ventilation hood with a strong fan.

▲ **THE COOKING AREA IN THIS DIMINUTIVE BUT VERY ELEGANT KITCHEN** is all business, with little floor space for extra bodies or countertop space for excess clutter. The small stovetop and microwave with built-in vent hood are stainless steel, as are the other appliances and built-in wine cooler.

◄ **WITH ALL THE CHARM OF A COLORFUL PAINTING,** this festive cooking area is contained in its own tile-covered alcove, which provides light, ventilation, and a sense of privacy. A metal rack keeps an entire set of copper pots at hand—a touch that's both practical and decorative.

▼ **DESIGNED WITH AN EYE FOR ARCHITECTURAL DETAIL,** all the elements of the cooking area in this small kitchen form a harmonious whole: stainless steel cooktop, tile backsplash, and roof-like ventilation hood with corbels and a chimney that exits through a cornice.

◀ **HOW NICE—AND PRACTICAL**—would it be to have all the spices you need right next to the stove? This innovative pullout, disguised as a pilaster that frames one side of the cast-iron range, slides out to reveal three narrow troughs, perfectly sized to hold spices and seasonings.

▲ **A CORNER CABINET PULLOUT** is a good substitute for a conventional lazy Susan. This kind of drawer arrangement allows cabinet contents to be diagonally pulled out of the cabinet, making kitchen utensils or food supplies very easy to access.

Hardware for Pullouts

A PULLOUT ALLOWS YOU TO LITERALLY PULL the contents out of a cabinet, where things are easier to see and access. Pullouts can be sized and designed to hold anything, from a compost bin to a toaster oven to a mixer. Unlike a drawer, a pullout can have more than one level. For example, a tall, narrow pullout may have three or four trays that hold spices or canned goods, stacked one above the other. In addition to ready-made pullouts available from catalogs and home supply stores, you can order custom pullouts tailored to your exact storage needs and the dimensions of new or existing cabinetry.

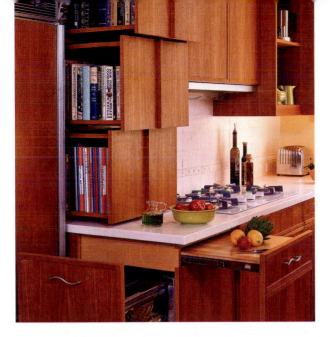

◄ PULLOUTS AREN'T JUST FOR LOWER-CABINET STORAGE. This kitchen features a pullout cutting board, multiple upper-cabinet pullout bins used to store books, and a large pullout storage unit at the end of the lower cabinet. When shut, pull-outs help maintain this kitchen's clean, modern look.

▼ SLIDING OUT ON WOODEN FRAMES supported by full-extension metal drawer glides, these woven basket pullouts are designed to hold potatoes, onions, and vegetables. The baskets provide well-ventilated, not to mention stylish, storage that helps keep their contents fresh.

Islands

UNLIKE LONELY TROPICAL ISLANDS in the middle of the ocean, kitchen islands are usually busy centers of activity where family members and guests prepare and eat meals, wash dishes, or just congregate and chat. In its simplest form, a kitchen island is just a lower cabinet that's in the middle of the kitchen area and not joined to other cabinetry. But in addition to providing a countertop work area that's easy to access from all parts of the kitchen, islands usually house a sink and/or cooktop or other appliance. An island with a built-in sink is a particularly good choice for a kitchen lacking windows, as a person washing dishes at an island faces out into the room rather than a wall of cabinets. A cooktop mounted in an island cabinet makes it easier to be with guests during meal preparation. And by adding a counter or small table surface to one side of an island, you can use it as an eating area or a place to serve hors d'oeurves and cocktails.

▲ KITCHEN ISLANDS AREN'T JUST FOR FOOD PREPARATION. Add a few chairs, and the island counter becomes a small dining table. The countertop of this island cantilevers out beyond the cabinetry, providing knee clearance for more comfortable seating.

◀ **WHILE A STURDY COUNTERTOP IS A MUST**, the lower portion of a kitchen island's cabinetry can be configured with any combination of drawers, doored compartments, pullouts, cubbies, or open shelves to suit the tastes and needs of its users.

▶ **TROPICAL ISLANDS AREN'T RECTANGULAR**, and kitchen islands don't have to be, either. While the kitchen side of this granite-topped, contemporary island is squared off, the other side offers a uniquely curved design, with three ample drawers flanked by open shelves.

◀ **BESIDES OFFERING AN EXCEPTIONAL AMOUNT OF COUNTER SPACE**, a kitchen island also makes a good location for a kitchen sink, range, or cooktop. This allows a host to be more sociable while preparing dinner—a great idea since family and guests tend to congregate in the kitchen.

▼ THIS LARGE ISLAND HAS ALL THE ELEMENTS of an entire kitchen and dining area in one unit: It provides a sink, cooktop, warming oven, and wine cooler in or below a stainless steel countertop that cantilevers out to form a small, glass-decked dining table.

▲ THIS LEGGED CABINET OFFERS THE LOOK of a freestanding table with all the sturdiness of a built-in (its legs are fixed to the floor). Employed as a stylish kitchen island, the cabinet's top is split: two-thirds wood countertop, one-third stone sink surround. Keep in mind that the plumbing will be visible under this type of built-in.

▲ IT ISN'T ALWAYS NECESSARY TO MATCH THE COLOR—or the exact style—of an island with the existing kitchen cabinets. This green-painted island's neo-classical details are fancier than the plain wood frame-and-panel kitchen cabinets surrounding them, but the contrast is appealing.

▶ SEPARATING THE KITCHEN FROM THE DINING AREA, the island in this painted kitchen has a bank of drawers on one side, useful for keeping silverware, placemats, and serving pieces, and a small wine rack on the other, separated by a kneehole that provides space for a chair or stool.

Eating Spaces

THESE DAYS, PEOPLE WILL EAT JUST ABOUT EVERYWHERE: in a car, on a ski slope, in front of the TV. But no home is complete without one particular area that's dedicated to dining. Whether it's a formal dining room, a cozy breakfast nook, or a kitchen alcove, an eating space should be set up to make eating convenient and comfortable. Of course, built-in furnishings can really help. In a formal dining room, a breakfront cabinet will keep all of your fine dishes, silverware, placemats, and glassware safe and organized, and make setting the table easier. With padded benches and ample table surface, a built-in breakfast nook is an efficient and appealing place to have daily meals with the family, without the space-soaking clutter of numerous chairs. And for a place to grab a quick bite or midnight snack, nothing beats a simple counter or bar that's part of a kitchen peninsula or island cabinet.

▼ **WHEN IT'S TIME FOR A QUICK BITE,** this diner-counter treatment is just the ticket. The elevated wood counter, set opposite the kitchen side of a long, narrow island, has enough room for several place settings, with plenty of space below for several stools or tall chairs.

◄ **THE EPITOME OF SIMPLE ELEGANCE,** this small pedestal table butts up to a shallow wall unit, complete with flanking columns, display shelves, and built-in lighting. The narrow two-seat table has a flip-up top extension to create space for additional diners.

▲ **HERE'S A ROCK SOLID IDEA:** The living room side of this kitchen peninsula cabinet is faced in the same rock as the adjacent wall, creating visual continuity between kitchen and adjoining room. The extended countertop is perfect for informal dining or a spread of hors d'oeuvres.

▲ **THE CHAIRS, TABLE, WALL CABINETS, LIGHT FIXTURES, CURTAINS, AND UPHOLSTERY** all work in concert with these built-in bench seats to create an everyday dining area that's warm and inviting. The finials on the posts of the curved-rail bench echo similar finials on the chairs for a unified but still eclectic look.

▲ **SINCE MEALS IN A CONTEMPORARY HOUSEHOLD** are often taken on the run, the overall plan for eating areas should include a spot in the kitchen as well as more formal areas. Spaces that are part of the kitchen, such as peninsula and island cabinets, provide convenient surfaces for snacks and quick meals.

◄ **ADDING A CABINET WITH COUNTER-TOP** or built-in table to a window bay is a terrific way to create an eating area with a view. This wood-topped cabinet completely fills the shallow bay and has ample knee room for comfortable seating.

Space Requirements for Eating Areas

FOR A BUILT-IN TABLE or breakfast nook to be comfortable and functional, it has to fulfill some basic ergonomic requirements. First, any table used for dining should be between 29 in. and 31 in. high. The table's apron (the frame that supports the top) should leave at least 24 in. of knee clearance underneath it.

Benches and seats should be about 21 in. deep (front to back edge) and may vary in height from 16 in. to 19 in., depending on the height of the table. If moveable seating is used, it's important to leave at least 36 in. of clearance between the table and any obstacles (for example, a cabinet or wall).

▲ **DIVIDING THE SPACE BETWEEN** food preparation and food serving areas is important, even for informal eating spaces. The raised beam and hanging pots on this island break up the large open space in this high-ceiling room and create a frame for the eating counter.

▲ THIS BREAKFAST NOOK TAKES ADVANTAGE of the kitchen's view of the woods. The arrangement of two bench seats facing each other across a trestle-style rectangular table creates a friendly space for eating a meal and carrying on conversation.

◄ WHETHER FOR BETTER OR WORSE, television is as much a part of informal dining today as the meal itself. The slight angle of the bar/counter in this modern home allows diners to easily see the TV in the built-in cabinet next to the kitchen area.

▲ **A HOME BAR IS THE IDEAL PLACE** to entertain guests as they sit comfortably while sipping a fine wine and noshing a sumptuous snack. The extended base cabinets and columns do a nice job of incorporating this long, elegant bar counter with the rest of the interior.

Dining Tables

IN ITS SIMPLEST FORM, a dining table need be little more than a flat horizontal surface. It should be sturdy enough to support heavy dishware and the weight of someone using it to lean on while standing. Size wise, a good general guideline is that every person sitting at the table should have a 24-in.-wide area.

If you're pressed for space but still have room to accommodate it, a built-in table can be a good solution. One of the long ends is usually attached directly to a wall, supported by a wide wooden cleat screwed directly to the wall or to a window frame (see the photo below). The other end can be attached to cabinetry, an opposite wall (in the case of a table built into an alcove), columns or posts in the room, or it can be supported with standard table legs.

▲ A BUILT-IN DINING TABLE IS NOT ONLY PRACTICAL, but it also can enhance the aesthetic appeal of a space and make it feel more user friendly. This two- or three-seat table was cleverly hung from the house's wood support posts on one side and window trim on the other.

DINING ROOMS

◄ **DETAILS ARE ESSENTIAL** when it comes to creating a stylish atmosphere in a formal dining area. The ambiance of this colonial-style dining room benefits from a number of successful built-ins, including a large, traditional fireplace and open-shelf cupboard.

▲ **BUILT-IN CABINETRY AND LIGHTING** play an important role in establishing a consistent style in any interior space, including the dining room. The clean-lined, veneered cabinet in this ultra-modern home divides the dining room from the kitchen and ties in with the natural wood floors.

▲ BECAUSE OF THE STORAGE IT OFFERS, cabinetry built into the dining room is always functional, but it also can contribute to the room's overall ambiance. The form and trim of this pair of arched-top hutches complements the formal colonial interior, as do the fancy china plates on display.

▲ BUILT-INS DON'T HAVE TO ACTUALLY BE IN THE DINING ROOM to be useful. This narrow wine rack is built into the wall just steps away from the formal dining area, connected through a dramatic, arched doorway. The wine is easily accessed, but the rack doesn't clutter the diners' view.

▲ **LOW, GLASS-DOORED CABINETS** topped by columns separate the front hall from the formal dining room of this home, while maintaining an open feel. The mullions on the cabinet doors echo the window frame treatments, while the tapered "battered" columns match those used on the outside of the house.

▲ **THE MATERIALS, DESIGN, AND DETAILS** of this craftsman-style, built-in hutch were carefully chosen to harmonize with the dining set. Recessing the cabinetry into the wall saved a substantial amount of open floor area, making the room feel more spacious and easier to maneuver in.

▲ A FORMAL DINING ROOM doesn't have to be overly formal. Built-in, bench-like seating wraps around a trestle table, creating this home's casual but elegant dining area. One section of the U-shaped bench is shorter than the other, extending only as far as the kitchen counter that it butts up to, adding visual interest and maneuverability.

► SEPARATED FROM THE KITCHEN by a built-in counter, this dining room is surrounded by windows with trim made from the same kind of wood. The trim treatment is continued around the room's high ceiling and helps tie the entire space together visually.

CORNER CABINETS

▲ THE CORNER OF A DINING ROOM is a great place to add a built-in without taking up valuable floor space. This corner cupboard's clamshell soffit and fluted side columns suit the colonial theme of the room perfectly, as does the antique-looking paint, which matches the room's wainscoting.

▲ IN A SMALL ROOM, the space between a corner and a feature, such as a fireplace or window, is an ideal place to squeeze in a built-in cabinet. This arch-topped hutch has glass-enclosed display shelves above a bank of drawers that are useful for storing flatware and table linens.

▼ OLDER HOMES BUILT AND FURNISHED in neoclassical styles, such as Federal and Georgian, are natural candidates for elaborate built-in cabinetry. This decorative corner cupboard was recessed into a diagonal wall in one corner of the dining room, thus enhancing its presence.

Bathrooms

BUILT-IN CABINETRY is an essential component of every bathroom, offering both practical storage space and visual appeal. Not only does it frequently provide housing for plumbing and fixtures, as in the case of a vanity or tub enclosure, but it also keeps a bathroom's contents handy, organized, and discreetly stored.

There are several different kinds of built-ins to consider when planning a bathroom. One of the most prevalent and basic is the vanity cabinet, which provides a mount for the sink, as well as extra counter space, drawers, and enclosed shelving for toiletries, cleaning supplies, and linens.

In a small bathroom, the vanity may provide the only storage space, but there are other possibilities that can help a cramped bathroom run more smoothly, including shelves mounted directly to a wall, cubbies in an alcove, or a recessed medicine chest. If you have the room, a built-in bank of drawers or a wardrobe-style cabinet lends style and capacious storage that can handle any household's demands.

The tub enclosure is another important bathroom built-in, which can add luxury as well as extra counter space. For maximum impact, the design and materials selected for a tub or whirlpool enclosure should complement the built-ins and trim used in the rest of the bathroom.

◄ **A BATHROOM VANITY DOESN'T HAVE TO LOOK** like a standard cabinet with a countertop. Constructed from thick hardwood that matches the paneling above the tub, this boxlike stand supports two top-mounted sinks and has a pair of flush-front drawers below.

Sinks & Vanities

SINCE THE EARLY DAYS of indoor plumbing, sinks and the vanities that hold them have become the focal points of the bathroom. While some styles of sinks, such as pedestals, are designed to stand alone, most are mounted atop a vanity. A good vanity serves several useful purposes. First, it's a secure platform that supports the sink and the faucets and drain that service it, while hiding the plumbing. Second, it creates a counter surface adjacent to the sink, which is useful for keeping brushes, cosmetics, shaving kits, and other toiletries close at hand. Last, but not least, a vanity provides space for storing all the sundry tools and supplies that keep us (as well as our bathrooms) clean and neat. In addition to its functional role, a vanity also is frequently the focal point of a bathroom; select its size, style, and finish to enhance the visual appeal of the space.

◄ BUILT TO RESEMBLE a freestanding piece of furniture, this unusual vanity creates an old-fashioned look in a bathroom that's otherwise contemporary in design. The mirror and medicine cabinet are made from a dark hardwood that matches the vanity.

▲ WHEN DECIDING ON A VANITY, it's important to choose a design and materials that complement the sink and fixtures as well as other furnishings and the overall style of the bathroom. This sleek, white vanity is in keeping with the rest of this modern bath, and its raised countertop shows off the under-slung glass sink to best advantage.

▲ TO INTEGRATE THE LOOK OF THIS VANITY with the rest of the room, the enclosure for the bathtub was constructed using the same dark-stained wood. Even though the vanity offers ample storage, recessed shelves above it provide easy access to fresh towels.

▶ **USING THE SAME TYPE OF WOOD AND FINISH** on this bathroom's vanity, medicine cabinet, shelf nook, and molding around the room's recessed ceiling produces a consistent appearance that ties the room together with the rosy-colored countertop and ceramic tile.

▼ **HAVE A SMALL BATHROOM** you don't want to overcrowd with a huge vanity? Using a small desk-style vanity with an open base, as these homeowners did, will give you a sink and counter space, as well as a modicum of storage, without taking up a lot of floor space.

▼ PEDESTAL AND SUSPENDED SINKS have very small footprints, making them a great choice for small bathrooms. Flanking this kind of sink with a pair of tall, drawered cabinets provides a place to stow toiletries and linens and adds a bit of counter space.

▲ WELL-DESIGNED BATHROOM VANITIES not only add storage and counter space, but a decorative flair as well. Witness the way this pair of striking sink cabinets is bridged by a lower counter and drawer, creating both visual interest and a perfect spot for applying makeup.

▼ THIS BATHROOM'S MEDICINE CHEST, wainscoting, and window trim are all made from the same wood as the vanity cabinet. The towel rack is a clever detail, made by widening the windowsill beyond the casing, then cutting a 2-in.-wide slot in it.

▲ BUILT FROM A WARM-COLORED EXOTIC WOOD called anigre, this elegant bathroom vanity has a subtly curved front that coordinates with the room's convex ceiling and round vanity mirror. Anigre was also used to panel the wall above the vanity's concrete countertop and slate backsplash.

Tub Enclosures

UNLESS YOU CHOOSE A FREESTANDING TUB for your bathroom, you'll need to create some kind of built-in enclosure around it. The style of tub you choose, its location, and the size and layout of the bathroom will affect the type of enclosure. For example, if you want a tub in the middle of the room under a skylight, you'll need a big space to accommodate the sizeable, box-like base required. In more modest baths, a tub against a wall with a partial enclosure is a more space-saving approach. Regardless, the enclosure can add style to the bathroom, complementing other fixtures: It can be painted, left with a natural wood finish, or covered with stone or tile. Also consider specific design details: A wide rim on the base provides a ledge for sitting or setting a bottle of bubble bath, and a ledge or built-in steps also make it easier to get in and out—especially with deep whirlpool- or Japanese soaker-style tubs.

▼ BY BUILDING THE RIGHT KIND of enclosure to suit your fixtures, you can add a tub practically anywhere in the bathroom—just remember to take into account the size and layout of the space. Freestanding on three sides, this simple box-type enclosure is covered with stone tiles that match the elegance of the room.

▶ NO PLACE TO RUN THE PLUMBING for the bathtub faucet? One solution is to mount the fixture directly on the enclosure—here, a small cabinet flanking the tub. There's still enough room left in the cabinet for a small drawer to hold shampoo and other bath supplies.

▶ FITTING THE BATHTUB INTO ITS OWN ALCOVE creates an intimate bathing space in this large bathroom. Using amber-colored hardwoods for the side of the tub enclosure, the vanity, and other bathroom furnishings provides a warm contrast to the room's cool green walls.

Shelving and Storage

I F YOUR BATHROOM VANITY **is bursting beyond capacity with shampoo, towels, toothpaste, cleansers, and such, adding shelves and storage cabinets can ease the overflow. In a large bathroom, a single built-in or freestanding cabinet provides oodles of clean, dry storage space. If floor space is minimal, utilize the area between wall studs to create a recessed chest or open-shelf storage. An even simpler solution is to mount a few shelves directly to the wall wherever there's room.**

▲ **THE ARCHED TOP AND CLEAN LOOK** of this recessed shelf unit echoes the neoclassical style of the bathroom. The clear glass shelves are great for display as well as storage, and they're easy to keep clean.

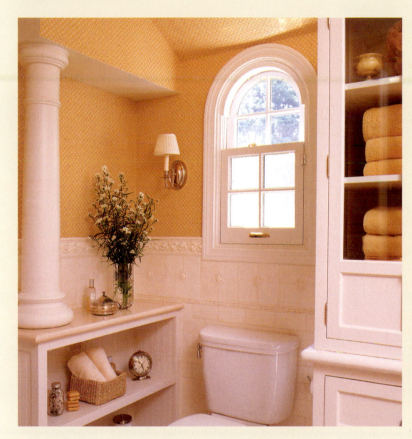

▲ **IN A SMALL BATHROOM,** any space is a good candidate for adding shelves. Open shelves on one side of the toilet are great for keeping toiletries handy, while the doors and drawers of the enclosed cabinet on the other side keeps towels and linens dry.

► **A SIMPLE ADDITION TO ANY BATHTUB ENCLOSURE,** these narrow box-beam shelves are attached directly to the wall above the tub. They're a handy place to keep bath salts, shampoo, and, of course, dry towels. Using the same material for the enclosure, wall, and shelves creates a unified look.

▲ TO MAINTAIN THE SENSE OF OPEN SPACE in this bathroom, the tub enclosure was built just high enough to accommodate the height of this classy teak bathtub. Covered with the same green marble as used on the floor and countertop, the wide lip of the enclosure provides a ledge to sit on and makes it easier to get in and out of the tub.

▶ LOCATING THIS TUB IN A CORNER OF THE BATHROOM where the ceiling drops down is a good use of space, taking advantage of an awkward nook while also conserving space in the rest of the room. The tub's thick ledge provides a place to sit or set toiletries.

◄ **LOCATING THE BATHTUB** next to a window with a lovely view of the ocean almost makes it feel like you're bathing outdoors. The panels of the wood enclosure were painted a light shade of blue to echo the watery view. Curved trim at the corners matches the form of the curvaceous tub.

Living Spaces

WHETHER A LIVING ROOM, family room, great room, or den, a home's living spaces are multipurpose destinations for family members and friends. They're places to congregate and do things, like watch a ball game or movie on TV, play a board game, or share good conversation and a snack.

Bookcases, display cabinets, shelving, fireplaces and mantels, window seats, and other built-ins all play a role in making our living spaces more functional and attractive. They can provide storage for sewing supplies or a place to show off a trophy, create a place to sit and read a magazine, or generate heat and add a cozy atmosphere. Built-ins are also useful for defining wall space or for dividing large open spaces into smaller private areas, say to allow video-game playing in one part of a family room without disturbing conversation in another.

Whether painted or made from natural wood, built-ins should enrich the ambiance of our living spaces. Because they're a central element of a room, it's important to carefully consider options when selecting built-in components to ensure they suit the style of the space, as well as work harmoniously with the room's fixtures and moveable furnishings.

◄ **THE GLASS DOORS ON THE CABINETS** flanking the fireplace are a perfect architectural echo of the mullioned semicircular window above, as well as the other windows in the room. This subtle repetition lends a unified sensibility to the room and places the focus on design rather than furnishings.

Fireplaces

WHEN IT COMES TO FIREPLACES, you could say, "home is where the hearth is." Whether it's part of a living room, den, or study, a hearth brings a warmth and charm that are easy to appreciate, especially on a cold winter's night. Most fireplaces are relatively simple forms, usually constructed from brick or metal with a chimney that may be hidden or exposed to the room's interior. However, a great deal of the charm of a fireplace installation is the way it's built into the room, so give it careful thought. A basic fireplace surround frames the hearth and provides a mantel shelf, which is a perfect spot to display photos, trophies, and other knickknacks. More elaborate designs can make a fireplace part of built-in cabinetry that takes up an entire wall. Such large built-ins not only provide living areas with useful storage and display space but also can serve as the focal point of an entire room.

▼ **A FIREPLACE NEED NOT BE SUR-ROUNDED** by blank wall space. Flanking this contemporary fireplace with natural-finished wood shelves and lower cabinets sets off the texture of the stone. In lieu of a mantel, the wall above also provides a place to display small artwork and other items.

▲ **A TASTEFUL FRAME-AND-PANEL WOOD FIREPLACE** surround creates a mantel that's more than twice as wide as the fireplace itself and incorporates a pair of twin-doored cabinets on either side. This design enhances an otherwise simple fireplace on a plain wall.

◄ **ONE STRATEGY TO CONSIDER** when creating or remodeling a fireplace is to add built-in cabinetry and paneling to an entire wall and integrate the fireplace into the complete treatment. The side panels of this fireplace incorporate padded wooden benches as well, creating a cozy nook by the fire.

▲ **IN THE CENTER OF A CONTEMPORARY HOUSE,** this raised fireplace hearth has a built-in bench on one side and a padded seating surface on the other, with convenient log storage below it. The light-colored tile and painted wood create a compelling contrast with the natural wood used elsewhere in the room.

▶ THIS ROOM EXEMPLIFIES A SUBTLE
WAY of incorporating built-in cabinets
into the same wall as the fireplace. The
design features glass-doored cabinets
above the mantel and painted cabinets
below, offering both visible display
storage and practical closed-door
storage.

◀ IN THIS VICTORIAN-STYLE HOME
with eye-catching coffered ceilings,
a built-in high-backed bench and
grilled room divider set the fireplace
area apart from the stairs, yet allow
heat to pass through the latticework
at the top. The bench also offers
comfortable seating around
the hearth.

▲ HERE, THE FIREPLACE IS JUST ONE COMPONENT of a large, multifunction, built-in cabinet that holds books and various display items. The narrow wood trim around the doors and ceiling was chosen to match the cabinetry and help blend it into the rest of the room.

▶ KNOTTY PINE WAS USED TO TIE THE LOOK of this classy, country-style interior together. The wood was used not only for the simple fireplace surround and mantel, but also for the bookcases in alcoves flanking the fireplace, the window frames, trim, and even the facings for the tie beams that span the room's open ceiling.

◄ **FOR A NEOCLASSICAL LOOK,** the two symmetrical cases framing this fireplace were given an arched, keystone top, recessed panels, and column-like side treatments. The treatments are repeated on a smaller scale on the sides of the fireplace surround.

▲ **DISPLAY CABINETS, FIREPLACE MANTELS** and other built-ins add warmth and style to living spaces. These cabinets nicely match the wood used for the room's windows, trim, and stairs, integrating the built-ins with the rest of the room.

▲ **WOOD ISN'T THE ONLY MATERIAL** to consider for built-ins! This entire fireplace wall was skillfully constructed from natural stone and two horizontal stone lintels. Various units for display and storage were also incorporated in the form of shelved recesses, closed cabinets, and a nook for firewood. The high window adds visual interest and lets in diffused light.

Woodstoves

IF YOUR HOME lacks a fireplace, adding a woodstove is the easiest way to gain both the symbolic and physical warmth that a hearth provides. Woodstoves can be installed practically anywhere in a room and produce more heat than typical fireplaces do. The hearth area built around the stove gives you an opportunity to use materials and design elements that enhance and harmonize with the surrounding space.

▲ USING THE BUILT-INS AROUND A HEARTH to continue an architectural theme or style that's already prominent in the room can make a striking statement. This Scandinavian-style hearth employs tiles and wood built-ins incorporating carved motifs to echo the room's coffered ceiling and rich color scheme.

▶ IF YOU HAVE ENOUGH STORAGE SPACE elsewhere, consider devoting the built-ins around a fireplace to seating instead. Doing so creates a cozy, intimate area and eliminates the need for multiple couches or extra chairs, leaving your living space more open and traffic flowing freely.

▶ **CABINETRY CAN HELP YOU INTEGRATE** both a fireplace and other architectural elements with the rest of the room. Here, a narrow case was fit between the fireplace and louver-shuttered window, with the case extending over the window to help frame it in the space.

▲ **THESE BUILT-IN BENCHES** create seating close to the fire as well as define and enclose the fireplace area. The benches, made of dressed stone to match the fireplace, are topped with wood and strewn with pillows for greater comfort and visual warmth.

◄ THIS HOME'S TWIN-SIDED FIREPLACE was incorporated into a large built-in unit that acts as a focal point for the room. The lower cabinetry flanks each of the two fireplace openings with twin-doored compartments, while the ends of the upper open shelf areas have elegantly curved sides, making the large unit seem less bulky.

▼ HAVE MORE TO DISPLAY in your living room or den than a narrow mantel can hold? A pair of clean, simple, open-shelved units on either side of the fireplace provides plenty of room to show off a family's treasures without standing out too much.

▲ CLEAR-GRAINED OR PAINTED WOOD would have seemed out of place around this rustic fireplace, so the mantel and built-in cabinetry were constructed from more primitive looking wood, rife with knots and quirky grain. The wood's patina and dark color fit with the room's country scheme.

▲ MATCHING WOOD VENEERS lend an elegant look to the contemporary built-ins that cover this fireplace wall. Face-frame-less construction, full overlay cabinet doors, stone fireplace surround, and glass shelves help create a clean, seamless look.

▶ THIS ROOM'S EXPOSED BEAMS create a rectangular pattern on the wall, dividing the space into a pair of built-ins that flank the stone fireplace. Made from wood that matches the rustic look of the beams, both open-shelf cases are topped by windows that allow heat to flow into an adjacent room.

◄ **BUILT-INS DON'T ALWAYS HAVE TO** precisely match the style of other architectural elements in a room. As an example, this traditional neocolonial fireplace surround is complete with capitol-topped columns and festoon surface decorations flanked by a less ornate and more contemporary-looking cherry wood built-in.

► **DON'T BE AFRAID** to finish cabinetry in bold colors if they harmonize with your decor. These built-ins make a strong and unique statement in this otherwise traditional room. The solid color also helps set off the features of the cabinet doors, arched alcove and desk, and mantel and fireplace surround.

Window Seats

EVEN IF YOUR HOME IS FURNISHED with lots of comfy chairs, a well-designed built-in window seat is a nice addition, as it offers more than just another place to sit. It can provide an inspiring view or be a getaway place with good natural light that's conducive to sewing or reading. Locating a window seat in an otherwise unused space—an odd-shaped alcove, a second-story dormer, or a deep window bay—can create an area that's open to the surrounding room, but has a sense of separation and privacy. It's also a smart and efficient way to make use of an awkward area. Window seats range from narrow, bench-like designs that provide extra seating for guests to L- or U-shape seating areas that create a conversation nook in a den or a reading area in a home library or study. Extra wide window seats can serve double duty as a daybed or extra sleeping spot for overnight guests.

▼ **EXPAND THE IDEA OF A SMALL WINDOW SEAT** and you get a wraparound couch, thus creating an intimate conversation area for family or guests. This room extension, surrounded on three sides with windows, was the ideal space for this kind of built-in seating.

A DORMER JUTTING OUT of a second story roofline offers the perfect spot for a window seat—and a great way to use an otherwise ineffectual space. If the area is deep enough, you can even make the window seat wide enough to double as an extra bed.

MOST WINDOW SEATS ARE VERY EASY TO BUILD and integrate into an existing space. Good window candidates are those at the end of narrow rooms or large landings, like this one, where they can be built in on three sides; only the side of the seat that faces the room needs to have finished woodwork.

Storage in a Window Seat

A WELL-DESIGNED WINDOW SEAT can provide storage as well as seating; the box-like construction of the lower seat is an excellent place for a voluminous storage compartment. The two most popular ways to do this are either to make the seat a hinged lid that lifts up for access or to add one or two drawers on the front of the seat. The hinged lid option is easy to construct and works with either a solid wood or upholstered plywood seat. If you choose the drawer option, use high-quality drawer glides, preferably the full-extension type that allow the drawer to slide all the way out, for better access. It's also a good idea to make the drawers as deep as possible so they'll hold bulky items like blankets and towels.

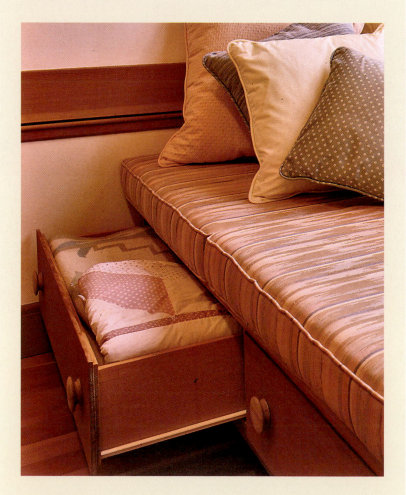

▲ ADDING LARGE DRAWERS to the lower portion of a window seat is an excellent way to gain additional storage. While you also can use the seat as a lidded box, drawers are much easier to access, especially for more frequently used items such as board games, DVDs, or extra blankets.

▼ TO PREVENT A WINDOW SEAT FROM LOOKING like it was just tacked on, look for ways to assimilate it more fully into the surrounding room. This contemporary seat has lower drawers that look like a continuation of the fixed cabinets around them, as well as a continuous sill that bridges the built-ins on both sides.

◄ **ONE WAY TO MAKE A WINDOW SEAT MATCH** the look of a colonial-style home is to add a spindled backrest. Although less comfortable than a padded rest, the curved back and spindles harmonize with the Windsor-style chairs and similar furnishings specific to that time period.

▲ **HAVE A LARGE, CURVED WALL WITH LOTS OF WINDOWS?** How about a long, curved window seat that runs beneath them? This is an effective—and relatively inexpensive—way to add lots of seating to a large room, with every seat getting a little piece of the view.

▶ **NOT EVERY WINDOW SEAT** has to have a huge picture window above it. Smaller window spaces also lend themselves to the creation of comfy built-in seating, as was done in this small, curved-ceiling alcove that's part of a den. The small window lets in light, but its raised position creates a sense of privacy.

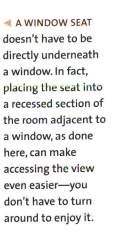
◄ A WINDOW SEAT doesn't have to be directly underneath a window. In fact, placing the seat into a recessed section of the room adjacent to a window, as done here, can make accessing the view even easier—you don't have to turn around to enjoy it.

◄ A WHITE-PAINTED FINISH helps tie the look of this window seat in with the built-in desk on one side and the pantry cabinet on the other. All three components are adjacent to the kitchen, which has cabinets that are also painted white for a unified look.

▶ BIG, FLOOR-TO-CEILING BUILT-IN CABINETS are great for all the storage space they provide, but they can create awkward spaces where cabinets stop and start at windows. A narrow window seat like the one shown here will not only span the gap but also add continuity between the lower cabinets.

▶ A BAY WINDOW IS A GREAT CHOICE for sitting a built-in window seat. Not only does the bay create an intimate space for the seat, but the transition between the bay and the surrounding wall gives you an opportunity to add trim that frames the entire seating area for added visual pizzazz.

Window Seat Placement

For best effect, a built-in window seat should be carefully located and oriented relative to its window. If the outside view is spectacular, make sure the seat faces it so sitters won't strain their necks to see out. If the window is small or if there is no view, orient the seat to provide good light for reading or sewing.

▲ WHO SAYS WINDOW SEATS ARE ONLY FOR SITTING? By making it wide enough, a single window seat or a U-shaped seating area like this can host multiple activities from conversation to cat-napping. The taller ends of these seats serve to partially separate the bay from the adjoining room.

▶ A DEEP RECESS FORMED BY A DORMER or window bay can feel like an entirely separate room. Built-in seating, curtain treatments, and wall decorations were used here to create a recessed window seat area with lots of privacy.

Entertainment Areas

W HETHER YOU LIKE TO WATCH OLD MOVIES, play video games, or read books, it's nice to have a comfortable place in the house in which to do it. One way to facilitate your passions and pastimes is to create a specific entertainment area in your home. If you have a large home, you might consider transforming an entire room into a home theater or library. Creating a media or reading area in an existing living space, say a den or family room, is a good alternative if space is at a premium.

In either case, built-in cabinetry will add aesthetic value and functionality to the space and can even section off an entertainment area from the rest of a large room. Cabinetry and built-in enclosures can house all the audio-visual electronics necessary for a good home theater system, offering tidy and efficient storage that's customized to your particular needs. Bookcases and shelf units provide a place to store and organize books, whether for a formal home library or a casual reading nook. Even if your home's entertainment area is simply a cozy corner, built-ins will maximize comfort and visual appeal.

◄ IF YOU'D RATHER PERUSE POE THAN STARE AT A SCREEN, a comfy reading spot is probably your idea of a home entertainment area. Plenty of shelves in a nearby built-in serve to keep a modest selection of your favorite books close at hand.

Media Centers

UNLIKE THE MORE GENERALIZED CABINETRY found in the rest of the house, built-ins made to house electronic components must be designed and constructed with special considerations in mind. First, the size and spacing of shelves, compartments, and cubbies must accommodate a range of audio-visual components (amplifiers, tuners, tape decks, VCRs, CD players and recorders, video game devices, etc.), which vary widely in dimension. Before customizing a built-in media center it's best to buy big items, such as wide-screen televisions, to confirm their exact space requirements. When in doubt, make an enclosure bigger—you can always add trim to conceal a gap. Because electronic devices generate heat when they're on, all cabinets with doors must allow air to circulate. Cabinets also must have correctly placed ports and pass-throughs for power cords, and for wires that connect components such as speakers, which may be located in a different part of the cabinet or room.

▼ CDS, DVDS, AND VIDEO GAMES all make for great entertainment, but they're best kept organized and stored out of sight when not in use. This customized built-in, which also features a large projection screen, has large, pull-out drawers and cabinets capable of housing a range of media.

▲▲ **THANKS TO A PAIR OF FLAT SLIDING DOORS** in this sleek cabinetry, the flat-screen television can do a disappearing act when it's not in use. This maintains a cleaner look in the room, and uncovers two banks of display shelves set on either side of the TV compartment. Leaving space around the screen protects it from heat damage due to the fireplace below.

▲ BALANCING FUNCTIONAL DISPLAY SPACE and closed storage is crucial when designing built-in cabinetry for entertainment areas. The solution here was to combine several large banks of drawers below with compartments for a television, stereo, and art displays above.

► THE SHEER SIZE OF A WIDE-SCREEN TV can easily overwhelm any modest-sized room. Recessing this screen into the wall surrounding it with trim and cabinetry that matches the room's Craftsman style décor de-emphasizes the screen's size and makes it feel integrated into the space.

◄▼ WHAT LOOKS LIKE A WALL OF LIBRARY CABINETS filled with books is actually a very clever built-in unit that houses a home entertainment center and bar. Sliding flipper doors, covered on the outside with faux book spines, retract to reveal the hidden compartments.

▼ Media center cabinetry need not be configured to hide electronic gear. If you like the clean, high-tech look of modern audio-visual components, consider incorporating them in such a way as to make them part of the over-all design.

▲ YOU DON'T NEED TO HAVE A SEPARATE ROOM to create a media center. This home's main living space pairs two seating areas with two focal points—a widescreen TV for relaxing and a fireplace for entertaining guests.

◄ A MEDIA CENTER DOESN'T NEED TO BE ENORMOUS to be right for its surroundings. This bedroom built-in accommodates a large television and electronic components and has a pair of retracting flipper doors that hide the components when they're not in use.

◄ ▼ **THIS NATURAL MAPLE ENTERTAIN-MENT CENTER** was designed to be tall and narrow so that it could be recessed into the wall to save space in the room. Open shelves on the sides of the unit store books, while two pairs of vertical pullouts provide storage for CDs and videotapes.

ELECTRONIC STORAGE

▲ THIS CABINET'S GLASS DOOR PROTECTS the electronic components inside from dust while reducing their visual impact in the room. The glass also allows the infrared beam of a remote control to pass through and operate components with the door closed.

▲ STACKING ELECTRONIC COMPONENTS on narrow shelves is a good way to pack a lot of gear into a tight space. This cabinet uses industrial-style rack-mounting hardware that firmly attaches each component to a pair of vertical metal rails on either side of the opening.

◄ ADDING NEW EQUIPMENT to an entertainment center is an all-too-common occurrence, as technology seems to upgrade daily. Fitting adjustable shelves inside an audio-visual cabinet makes it easier to incorporate additional components or reconfigure your system when needed.

Reading Spaces

WHILE ANY SPOT, from a porch swing to a bathtub, can be adapted for reading, true bookworms will derive great pleasure from having a comfortable place in their homes specifically designated as a reading area. Whether that space is a corner of the den, a separate home library, or a nook at the top of the stairs, it should be relatively quiet, well lit, and equipped with a cushy chair (or built-in window seat) and a bookcase or two, to keep reading materials organized and close at hand. Freestanding shelves are an easy, less expensive temptation, but in the long run, built-ins are usually more sturdy and command more presence in a room. Options range from wall-mounted shelving, to open bookcases with fixed or adjustable shelves (the latter being most flexible), to furniture-like bookcases with glass or wood-paneled doors that keep your most precious first editions clean and safe.

▼ HAVE ENOUGH BOOKS TO FILL A small library? Outfitting the walls of a den or spare bedroom with built-in bookcases can provide you with miles of shelves to house your collection and transform an otherwise ordinary space into a stately home library.

▲ **THE WARMTH OF WOOD IN A PANELED STUDY** lends itself perfectly to the addition of a built-in bookcase or two. Housing your finest volumes behind glass doors protects them from dust and smoke and makes even paperbacks appear more special.

▶ **MEZZANINES ARE A TERRIFIC PLACE** to add bookcases for a home library and reading area. Narrow bookcases along the walls provide space to store precious volumes while occupying little floor space and producing a dramatic visual effect.

Hardware for the Library

ADJUSTABLE SHELVES **are a** blessing when organizing books, which can range dramatically in size and shape. Adjustable shelf hardware varies too, from strong metal rail systems that support the weight of the largest tomes to pint-sized brackets that insert into ¼-in. holes drilled into the sides of the case and that support the shelf almost immediately.

◀ **DON'T OVERLOOK THE EFFECT** trim and fixtures have on built-in cabinetry. The thin molding trim, antique candle sconces, and pierced metal grill on the heat register (behind the bench) all work together to frame and accentuate these modest built-in bookshelves, making them appear more substantial and grand.

▲ YOU CAN USE CABINETRY TO DEFINE AND DIVIDE a large room into two or more separate areas. The pair of glass-doored peninsula cabinets shown here partially encloses the study and reading area. The peninsulas connect to taller book cabinets that line the side walls.

▶ IF A WALL-SIZED BOOKCASE is too dull and conventional for your tastes, consider cabinetry that adds shelf space yet integrates the room's architectural features and furniture. This well-proportioned built-in surrounds a doorway and has a seating nook, as well as plentiful shelving.

◄ **THE ADDITION OF A BUILT-IN BOOK-CASE** that surrounds a window helped define this space as a cozy reading nook. The nook was created during a remodel, when the hallway was widened by reallocating space from a bathroom and a deck.

◄ **AN ELEVATED WINDOW SEAT** provides an ideal reading and conversation area in this unique home library. The room's adobe construction and terra cotta floor tile create a southwestern feeling that's appropriate to the home's location in the mountains of New Mexico.

Bedrooms

I N ADDITION TO BEING WELCOMING AND COMFORTABLE, a bedroom or sleeping area in a contemporary home also needs to be practical and multi-functional. That's because we do a lot more in our bedrooms than just snooze.

At different times, a bedroom may function as a place to get dressed and undressed or try on new outfits; a comfy spot to lay down and read a book or cuddle with a loved one; a getaway place to listen to music or play a board game; or even a full-blown home theater where you can watch television or the latest movie while reclining in comfort. Now, more than ever, built-in cabinetry and furniture is an essential part of creating bedrooms that serve our diverse lifestyles.

Built-in cabinetry in the bedroom can help to tidy up and organize a room and use whatever space there is efficiently. For example, a wardrobe cabinet or armoire can add the closet space a bedroom may lack or create a dressing area with plenty of rack space and drawers for clothes. Or the look and utility of a master bedroom may center around a built-in bedstead, complete with integrated nightstands, under-bed storage, lighting, and perhaps even a television cabinet.

◄ THE BUILT-IN WINDOW SEAT, wainscoting, beams, and window trim are as much a part of this bedroom's pleasant ambiance as the furniture and fixtures. The white-painted woodwork and ceiling help keep the room bright, reflecting light from its many windows.

Sleeping Areas

A COMFORTABLE BEDROOM OR SLEEPING AREA requires more than just a patch of floor with a mattress on it. Well-designed sleeping spaces often integrate the bed into the room itself—for example, a bedstead built into an alcove or dormer. Built-in beds not only provide a place for a box spring and mattress, but for other amenities as well: drawers for bed linen or clothing; shelves for books, framed photographs, or small art objects, possibly with sconces or overhead lighting; night tables; even a footboard blanket chest or television cabinet. A wide window seat or pullout couch can serve as a convertible sleeping area for overnight guests.

▼ **WHAT MORE SOOTHING WAY** to start a new day than in a sleeping area surrounded by windows and greenery in a room doused in soft white hues? The ethereal effect is created by using white paint on all trim, baseboards, the built-in closet, and low cabinets.

▲ **BESIDES PROVIDING USEFUL STORAGE,** bedroom built-ins can define an entire sleeping area. These handsome, contemporary built-ins, made from matched wood veneers, create a unique bed surround with recessed lighting, drawered night stands, a headboard, footboard, and platform for the mattress.

◄ **JUST BECAUSE YOU SLEEP IN AN AREA** doesn't mean you can't read and relax there too. An arched alcove in this bedroom provides a cozy place to read before bedtime. A recessed shelf set into a short wall that divides the alcove from a closet provides space for a few books and knickknacks.

► **LIGHTING IS AN IMPORTANT PART OF ANY SLEEPING AREA.**
Building this unit into the wall provided the opportunity for
architectural interest as well as abundant lighting options.
The wall sconces add visual appeal and strong light perfect
for reading, while a fluorescent fixture hidden in a soffit
produces a more romantic, diffuse illumination.

▼ **LOW BUILT-IN CABINETS ARE GREAT
FOR STORING** bed linens as well as
clothes and personal items. The
drawered bank here wraps around the
room and runs beneath the window,
adding shelf space and concealing a
radiator; the louvered openings add
visual interest while controlling
the heat.

▲ WHEN DESIGNING OR REMODELING UPSTAIRS BEDROOMS, always look for ways to make the best use of reduced-headroom spaces that result from a sloping roofline. Here, built-in cabinets and drawers beneath the dormer windows take advantage of that otherwise wasted space.

◀ A CONSISTENT USE OF MATERIALS prevents this rustic sleeping area, set into a triangular window bay, from looking like a crude, unfinished space. The bed, blanket chest, and window trim are all made from the same construction lumber used to frame the room, producing a comprehensive—and striking—design.

NON-TRADITIONAL BEDS

▼ EVEN IF YOUR BEDROOM ALREADY HAS AMPLE AREA for a large bed, consider transforming an alcove into an additional bed by installing a wide, padded seat. The curtains added to this alcove may be drawn for privacy.

▲ MURPHY BEDS AREN'T JUST FOR SMALL URBAN HOTEL ROOMS any more! Electric raising and lowering controls on this modern Murphy make it a breeze to transform this bedroom's exercise space into a comfy sleeping area. The mirror on the panel conceals the bed, while being useful to check form during exercise.

▲ A BED DOESN'T HAVE TO BE a piece of freestanding furniture. These padded built-ins double as twin sofas in the daytime and beds at night. A small drawered unit at the end of each bed creates a headboard, while generous drawers beneath each bed store blankets and linens.

◄ A SINGLE, BOLD-BLUE BUILT-IN provides a closet, a chest of drawers, a
doored cabinet, and a top bunk-style
bed for this small bedroom with a high
ceiling. A ladder, secured by a rail that
allows it to be moved from side to side,
provides access to the lofty sleeping
quarters.

▼ A SINGLE, WELL-DESIGNED BUILT-IN can turn a small or
quirky portion of a room into a self-contained sleeping area.
This example provides a platform for a twin-sized bed with
multiple storage drawers underneath, a doored cabinet at
the head of the bed, and a small counter for a lamp, clock,
or flowers.

Entertainment Spaces

LONG GONE ARE THE PURITAN DAYS when bedrooms were only used for sleeping. A modern bedroom can be a place for entertainment as well as slumber. A well-appointed bedroom is a haven— a place to spend a little quiet time by yourself or watch a movie with a loved one. Built-in cabinetry figures prominently in adapting a bedroom for entertainment while maintaining a clean and stylish interior. For example, recessed lights in a wall-mounted headboard or soffit can provide light for reading or playing board games in bed. For listening to music or watching television, consider housing the television and stereo in an entertainment center built into a wall or corner of the bedroom. You can even hide the television set when it's not in use by enclosing it in a chest-like cabinet fitted with electric lift hardware that raises the TV up for viewing at the push of a button.

▼ **IF YOU LIKE TO WATCH TV IN BED**, consider incorporating a television into your bedroom built-in. Designed to coordinate with the room's other furnishings, this large wall unit offers lighting, display space, and storage, as well as a bedtime entertainment center.

◄ **AUTOMATED LIFT HARDWARE** is fantastic for creating pop-up furniture like this bedroom console, which conceals a large television and audio-visual components. At the push of a remote control button, the electric lift raises the television up into the viewing position.

▲▶ **THIS ROOM DIVIDER**, styled after a Japanese screen, provides chic housing for a movie screen—the projection television is mounted overhead. A cabinet below the screen holds the system's electronics.

Closets & Dressing Areas

HAVING ADEQUATE CLOSET SPACE to stack, stuff, or hang all the components of a modern wardrobe is essential for practical living. If your bedroom is short on closet space, creating a built-in wardrobe cabinet in a corner of the room or adding a multi-drawer dresser in an alcove or recess can provide the storage you need. If you have a little more space to play with, strategically placed cabinetry can divide open space and create dressing areas. Such areas are not only practical, but they also make changing clothes for work or play a more comfortable and private experience. If your bedroom already has lots of closet space, adding shelves, racks, bins, cubbies, and drawers can help keep clothes ordered and neat, and help you efficiently utilize every square inch of closet space. There's also a wealth of easy-to-install hardware designed specifically for organizing closet spaces.

▲ **DRESSING AREAS ARE IN LARGE PART DEFINED** by the built-in cabinetry that stores and organizes various wardrobe components. This wall unit, located in a narrow hallway opposite an open walk-in closet area, has oodles of drawers and cubbies, arranged symmetrically for his and her clothing.

◄ **IF YOU'RE A CLOTHESHORSE,** you'll want lots of storage space in the bedroom. Built-in, drawered chests such as these not only provide ample space to keep clothes, linens, and accessories, but they also help create a streamlined effect in a room by reducing the number of freestanding furniture pieces.

▲ ADDING BUILT-IN ARMOIRES AND WARDROBE CABINETRY is a good way to add necessary clothes storage to a bedroom with minimal or no closet space. A single cabinet can house rods for hanging clothes and storage cubbies and drawered chests for folded items.

▲ ONE WAY TO ENSURE THAT BUILT-IN CABINETRY fits into an interior is to match it with the materials, construction, and design of the surrounding doors, windows, and trim used in the space around it. The frame-and-panel wood drawer fronts on this chest harmonize with the style of the woodwork in the dressing area.

A WELL-ORGANIZED WALK-IN CLOSET is a thing of beauty. Here, separate built-ins were used for specific storage purposes. They include several banks of closets with rods for hanging clothes, a shoe rack and drawered chest on the opposite wall, and a large rack just for ties filling space at the end.

◄ **NO ROOM FOR A FULL CLOSET** in a teeny-tiny bedroom? No problem. Adding a bank of shallow built-ins on one wall can provide a decent amount of storage for clothing and linens without robbing much floor space.

▲ **TO GAIN FULL ACCESS TO THE CONTENTS OF DRAWERS,** always fit them with full-extension glide hardware. This is especially important on short drawers that can't be opened very far without extension hardware, such as these, which are part of a shallow, built-in dressing area.

◀ **EARLY AMERICAN HOMES RARELY HAD BUILT-IN CLOSETS**—their occupants kept their clothes in armoires and chests. An easy way to add a bedroom closet is to enclose one in a corner of a room. This simple closet and door were built from tongue-and-groove wood paneling.

▼ **TO MAINTAIN THE SLEEK, CLEAN LOOK** that's essential in a modern-style interior, full overlay cabinet doors and drawers were installed in this dressing area. The result is a flush-front built-in with only small pull knobs and narrow lines defining the cabinet's face.

Closet Organizing Hardware

IF THE CLOTHING AND LINENS piling up around your bedroom are making it look more like a gopher-infested garden than a tidy sleeping area, it's probably time to overhaul and reorganize your closet. Fortunately, modern closet hardware and accessories make this job easier than ever. Wire shelves, racks, bins, and pullouts are easy to install (mounting usually requires just a few screws) and quickly turn wasted and/or cluttered space into useful, organized storage.

▼ ECHOING THE GRAND STYLE OF EUROPEAN ARMOIRES and wardrobes made centuries ago, this contemporary built-in dressing cabinet features elaborately carved drawer pulls and moldings, painted decorations on its door panels, and even an inset clock in its arched top.

▲ A CORNER CABINET IS A PRACTICAL ADDITION that makes good use of an odd-shaped or limited-access space in a closet. Because it angles out toward the closet opening, this simple four-drawer, four-shelf chest is easy to access.

▲ **WELL-DESIGNED BUILT-INS** make the most of limited space in a small dressing area. This wardrobe closet effectively utilizes the area between its flat-panel door and the clothes racks and cubbies with a door-mounted shoe rack that swings out, providing easy access to more than a dozen pairs.

Kids' Rooms

The furnishings in a child's room must be functional, but kids' rooms also need to provide a comfortable, safe environment, with fixtures that make the room a fun place where your child will want to be—even at bedtime. Built-ins are an excellent addition to any furnishing scheme, providing efficient storage as well as infinite opportunities for kid-style creativity. Multipurpose built-in units are very useful in bedrooms that are small or shared by two or more children. For example, a single built-in can have storage shelves and drawers, a pair of fold-down desks, and twin bunk-style beds.

Unlike the designs of more formal spaces, kids' rooms are the most appealing when they incorporate a child's particular interests or unique visions. For example, a built-in bed platform can be designed to look like it's floating atop a flower-filled meadow, or a shelf unit can be made to look like stacked-up ABC blocks. Don't be afraid of using colorful finishes and incorporating decorative touches, such as murals or decals with favorite characters from storybooks, movies, or video games.

Whether play space is incorporated into a bedroom or has its own special place, built-in chests and bins provide attractive, efficient storage for games, toys, and art supplies.

◄ AS IN A KITCHEN OR LIVING ROOM, built-in furnishings not only provide useful surfaces and storage in a child's room, but they can also be employed to divide or define space within it. This low bookcase helps separate a child's sleeping space from the larger, adjacent play space.

Bedrooms

CHILDREN'S BEDROOMS have most of the same requirements that adult bedrooms do: a comfortable place to sleep, storage for clothing and linens, areas to display artwork and keep personal items, and perhaps a place to read and study. However, a cleverly styled and appointed children's bedroom is a lot more fun to be in; especially in younger children's rooms, there's less need to adhere to formal design constraints. If your child is a big sports fan, why not create a built-in bed, desk, and wall unit with colorful locker-room-style doors? Are trains your seven-year-old's favorite thing? Make them a recurring motif by using decals or stenciled train designs on the room's built-in cabinetry, as well as on the upholstery, curtains, and wall treatments. With a little effort, you can create a bedroom that's practical for everyday use while also being a welcome getaway for your child.

▲ A GRAPHIC TRAIN THEME UNIFIES this child's room, providing a simple way to jazz up the space. Using a decal of the motif on the dresser creates an intriguing three-dimensional effect and harmonizes the built-in with the rest of the room.

◄ THE CHALLENGE OF CREATING SPACE and privacy in a room shared by two children is more easily fulfilled with the use of carefully placed built-ins. Here, large bookshelves divide separate study areas from a window seat between them, and curtained alcoves create personal sleeping spaces.

▲ **NOTHING SAYS "KID'S SPACE"** better than a bright wall-paint scheme and colorful, playfully patterned cushions, curtains, and upholstery. The painted finish on this window bed's trim and cabinet platform, which provides handy storage, is durable and easy to clean.

▲ **CREATING A SEPARATE STUDY SPACE** in a child's bedroom is a good way to encourage positive homework habits. The alcove in this room was outfitted with a large desk (built to suit a child's stature) featuring twin drawer banks, which sits beneath a wall-mounted bookcase. All were painted to complement, rather than overwhelm, the room's delicate décor.

► THIS BED PLATFORM, BUILT-IN DESK, AND WALL UNIT create a sports theme (good if your child is a sports fan but fickle about favorites), which is echoed by the wallpaper trim. The padlocks and louvers on the desk and wall unit provide realistic detail.

◄ DESIGNING A KID'S ROOM provides an opportunity to let your imagination go. This bed platform, complete with built-in drawers and shelving, creates a fantastical environment suitable for sleep and play. The wall mural unifies the fairy theme while making this space truly special.

► FACED WITH AN ODD ROOFLINE that couldn't be modified, the builder decided to use the space to create an enclosure for a child's bed. The cozy corner bed has a recessed light above it and plenty of drawered storage in the platform that supports the mattress.

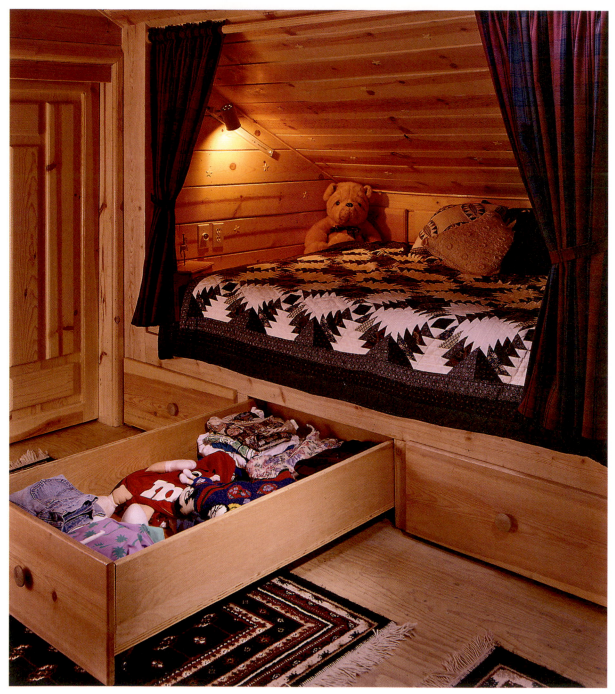

► THIS BUNK-STYLE CHILD'S BED takes advantage of reduced headroom space where the roofline slopes down. Large drawers that pull out from beneath the bed offer plenty of storage for clothing, bed linens, towels, and more.

Play Spaces

KIDS USUALLY DON'T NEED A LOT OF INCENTIVE to engage in play. What they do need, however, is a clean, safe place to play in. A play space may be in the child's bedroom or in a designated part of another living space, like a den or study. To make the space more inviting and practical, add built-in cabinetry such as benches and platforms for a raised play surface or seating. Shelves and bins provide storage for toys, books, and games when play is done, yet make it easy for children to access them when they want to. Enclosed cabinets are a good choice for shared living spaces, so you can store toys out of sight when adults take over the area. You can make a play area jollier by decorating the cabinetry with colorful drawer and door pulls, decals, or decoupage photos and imagery.

◄ **KEEPING TOYS OFF THE FLOOR** and neatly stored is the purpose of this inventive shelf unit, which is mounted on hinges and serves as a door between a child's room and an adjacent study and play area. When closed, the door/shelf melds with the two fixed shelves on either side of it.

▲ A WIDE, LOW BUILT-IN BENCH can provide not only seating and sleeping room, but play area as well. This long, L-shaped bench is high enough to work as a child's seat but not so high that it causes concern in case an overactive player takes a tumble.

▲ WANT TO ADD SOME COLOR to a child's play area or bedroom? You can do it by painting the built-ins or covering them with brightly colored plastic laminates, such as Formica, or solid-surface materials like Corian. Colorful walls and imaginatively patterned carpets are another possibility.

▲ **COMPLETE WITH DRAWERS BELOW** and shelves above, the
built-in cabinetry shown here provides a place to keep
junior's toys out of sight, thus reducing clutter. The soft yellow
color scheme is inviting for a young child but sophisticated
enough that it will work for an older child, too.

▲ **HERE'S A CLEVER IDEA:** a sliding dividing screen that can be maneuvered to partition off play space from the rest of the room. The two rolling screens hang on track hardware normally used for closet doors. One panel has a small window, and both have foot bolts to lock them down when in position.

◀ STUFFED ANIMALS, DOLLS, BOOKS, action figures, and art supplies all need a place to go when playtime is over. This colorful room has plenty of shelf space and cabinetry to provide storage for all these play things. Pink and yellow columns and applied surface decorations contrast boldly with the purple cabinetry.

▼ INSTALLED AROUND A PAIR OF WINDOWS in a small room, this built-in unit features padded seats and fold-down tables with storage cabinets below. The crenelated castle-like trim around the top of the unit adds a whimsical touch and provides a place to keep stuffed animals.

Using Kid-Friendly Materials and Surfaces

SHARP EDGES, SPLINTERS, AND TOXIC FINISHES **should all** be carefully avoided when building cabinetry and furniture for a child's room or play area. Solid surface materials, like Corian, plastic laminates, metals, and other inert materials are good choices. If solid wood is used, avoid species prone to splintering, such as Douglas fir, cedar, or redwood. Make sure to round all edges and corners generously, and sand all surfaces smooth. Finish raw wood with a few coats of mineral oil, any food-safe finish, or a coat of wax.

Workspaces

WHILE MANY OF THE ROOMS IN OUR HOMES are designed to accommodate socializing, fun, and entertainment, most homes also should have some kind of workspace. Depending on whether you earn your bread and butter via a home-based business or just need a place to spread out and practice your hobby, that place might be a formal home office or an informal work area.

The kind of furnishings and built-ins you need to support a home office obviously will depend on how you work and the equipment and supplies that you need. At a minimum, your office should have a comfortable work area with desk or counter, cabinetry to house electronic gear and equipment, and files and shelves for storage of papers, books, and supplies.

Ideally, an informal work area also should have adequate surface and storage space, supplied by both freestanding and built-in furnishings. If a work area takes up part of a living room or den, it's important to have easily accessible space to store your projects and supplies when guests are coming.

Whether for a home office or a more casual work area, any built-in cabinetry or shelving you choose to install should work harmoniously with the trim and architectural details in the surrounding space.

◄ **WHATEVER YOUR IDEA OF THE PERFECT WORKSPACE,** it's certain to have lots of storage that keeps books, files, papers, and other work-related materials organized and within easy reach. Open shelves that line three sides of a narrow, U-shaped workspace serve that purpose here.

Home Offices

WHETHER YOU'RE A WRITER, THERAPIST, OR TAX CONSULTANT, if you work in your house or apartment, you need a home office that's an efficient and comfortable place to conduct business. Privacy is the first issue. If your office isn't in its own room, a peninsula cabinet or a built-in divider can help separate it from the rest of the room. One of the most important things you'll need is a spacious work surface—a big desk, table, or countertop. Wall shelves and built-in cabinetry sized and proportioned to fit your space can house computers, copiers, fax machines, and whatever other equipment your job requires. You'll also need drawers for storing your paper files, drawings, and such. By carefully planning and laying out the cabinetry and furniture, and integrating it with the room's windows, lighting, and other features, your home office will not only be a relaxing and resourceful place to work, but it will be stylish, too.

◄ A SPACE SET UP FOR WORKING AT HOME should be functional and comfortable, but that doesn't mean it can't be stylish as well. This dark-stained-wood built-in wall cabinet and desk are neoclassically styled to match the home's décor. The cabriole-legged computer table fits right in.

▲ YOU'LL MAKE WORKING IN YOUR HOME OFFICE a cheerier experience by letting in lots of light. The desk surface in this bright, minimally decorated work area (a smart approach if you get distracted easily) was wisely positioned next to a window with a pastoral view.

▲ BUILT-IN CABINETRY PROVIDES A VISUAL FOUNDATION for creating an office or study area in your home. The office shown here is fashioned around a wall unit that displays art and fine books, adjacent to a bookcase placed below windows that are trimmed to match the built-ins.

▲ OPEN SHELVES ARE HANDY FOR QUICK ACCESS to books and papers but can have a cluttered appearance. Relegating storage of papers, binders, and loose items to drawers or shelves and pullouts housed behind cabinet doors will help keep your home office looking neat and tidy like this sleek, contemporary study.

▶ TO GIVE YOUR HOME OFFICE AN "EXEC-UTIVE LOOK," keep all the paperwork hidden in desks and drawers, and concentrate on creating an attractive, richly traditional space. These floor-to-ceiling built-ins have lots of well-lit shelves that show off small sculptures, trophies, and a few select books.

◀ WANT TO CREATE AN OFFICE WITH AN EXCITING MODERN LOOK? Choose materials that conjure an industrial or high-tech theme, such as unfinished steel for shelves and work counter frames, granite or solid-surface material for counters and desk surfaces, and tinted plastic for doors and drawer fronts.

▲ THE FOLD-DOWN, SLIDE-OUT DESK mounted on this built-in wall unit provides a writing surface, helping to transform an ordinary living space into a small home office. When the office isn't needed, the table folds away and doors shut to enclose the computer and printer.

▶ MODERN HOME OFFICES OFTEN NEED to accommodate many different kinds of work: writing, drawing, drafting, rendering artwork, computer work, and more. Here, a drafting table fills an angled corner between two built-in desks. The handy rolling taborette, just left of the drafting chair, makes supply storage a breeze.

Ventilation

PRACTICALLY ALL ELECTRONIC DEVICES give off heat when they're running. If such components are housed or enclosed in cabinetry, it's vital to provide ventilation so that the heat can escape. On most cabinets, this requires little more than cutting a few large holes or slots in the enclosure. If possible, cut openings near both the top and the bottom of the unit. This allows cool air to enter at the bottom and hot air to exit at the top. If the openings will show, you can dress them up by installing louvered or screened covers made of plastic or metal.

▼ TO HIDE THE UGLY GRAY HOUSINGS of computer monitors or industrial black of televisions, consider building them into home-office cabinetry. The monitor pod atop this pentagonal, custom desk not only conceals the monitor but also shields its screen from annoying glare, while the television can easily be tucked away when not in use.

► **PRACTICALLY ANY HOME OFFICE CAN BENEFIT** from having more shelf space for books and periodicals. An alternative to using shelves and bookends is to create storage cubes, as shown here. They allow the removal of a volume or two without upsetting an entire shelf.

◄ **ONE WAY TO GAIN MORE SPACE** in a small home is to remodel the attic into a bedroom or home office. This remodeled attic features a built-in desk and drafting table, installed under a shed-style dormer that provides headroom. Open shelves along one side of the attic offer ample storage and display space.

Work Centers

BUILDING MODEL AIRPLANES, sewing quilts, collecting stamps; all these pastimes have one thing in common: They're most comfortably performed in a home work center. Of course, the business of life, including bills and taxes, also benefits from a designated workspace. Unlike a home office that's set up for daily formalities, a work center is intended for more casual use, in the evenings or on weekends. The idea is to have a desk or counter where you have plenty of room to spread out your work, with drawers and cabinetry close at hand to neatly store all the supplies you need. If space is cramped, a single built-in unit with a counter or flip-down desk and with drawers and cabinet space can do the trick (just make sure there's plenty of good lighting). You might also add shelves to your work center for books, art, or to proudly display your creations.

▼ ANY WELL-DESIGNED PIECE OF BUILT-IN CABINETRY should work harmoniously with the trim and architectural details of the surrounding space. These built-in cabinets and home work center fit in beautifully with the rustic beam construction of the room.

▲ **WHEN YOU NEED A PLACE TO WORK,** any available space makes a good candidate. One advantage of outfitting a work area with custom built-ins is that they may be designed to suit an oddly shaped or proportioned space, such as this corner of an upstairs bedroom.

Media Storage

IF YOU WORK WITH A COMPUTER, you undoubtedly have lots of discs that contain impor-tant files. Although newer optical media, including CD-ROM and DVD discs, have a longer life expectancy than magnetic media (floppy discs and backup tapes), it's a good idea to create some kind of media storage in your home office or work area. It's best to store media in a cabinet with doors that reduces exposure to light and mois-ture. Whatever design you choose, plan ahead to ensure that you have enough room for current and future archives.

▲ IT DOESN'T TAKE MUCH IN THE WAY OF CABINETRY to create a small, but useful, multipurpose work area. In this example, a closet was transformed into a work nook, with shelves for a computer and stereo, and a desk surface. A low bookcase provides storage and separates the area from the home's entryway.

◀ A SLOPING ROOFLINE usually forms upstairs spaces with reduced headroom. These are great locations to build in a counter, desk, and cabinets to create a work area. The counter shown here narrows at one end to create clearance for open drawers in the storage cabinet.

▼ BUILT LIKE A SHALLOW DRAWER and mounted on sturdy, full-extension drawer glides, this clever pullout desk provides a handy writing surface for this room's work center. A recessed counter and pigeonholes lend space to store papers, staplers, and other desk accessories.

▲ **TO MAKE THE MOST OF THE TALL, NARROW SPACE** in this small room with a peaked ceiling, a long bookcase and recess were added between the windows. The work area's L-shaped desk features a drafting table, a deep drawer bank, and a pullout tray for the computer keyboard and mouse.

▼ THIS SMART, CONTEMPORARY-STYLE WORK AREA exemplifies a classic workspace design formula, featuring a small desk and lower cabinet below a case with shelves and cubbies for books and other items. The lower rail of the case conceals a recessed fluorescent fixture that lights the desk area.

▲ AREAS ADJOINING THE KITCHEN or dining area are prime spots for adding a workspace. When installing cabinets and counters adjacent to kitchen cabinetry, either use the same design or a complementary one to ensure visual flow. You also can designate some of the shelves in the work area to store cookbooks or display fancy dishware.

◄ LARGE, SHALLOW DRAWERS are a great addition to a work area built-in, especially if you collect maps, photographs, artwork, stamps, or other flat objects. The cabinetry shown here has space and storage designed to accommodate an artist's needs.

► WHEN YOU DESIGN YOUR OWN WORK AREA with built-ins, you can add as many cabinets, drawers, and features as you need. This small work area built around a window has plenty of drawers with divided compartments for supplies, and lots of counter space and shelves to display completed artwork and knickknacks.

Workspaces | 159

▶ **THIS SIMPLE DESK** was created from a countertop mounted on a shallow box-like cabinet containing several drawers. One end of the desk attaches to a built-in bank of shelves that divides the kitchen from the rest of the room, and provides an additional work surface.

▶ **WHEN SEARCHING FOR A SPACE** in your home to turn into a small work area, be sure to look under the stairs—space that's often wasted. This attractive installation features a counter large enough to hold a computer with recessed lighting added to the ceiling above it.

▲ TUCKED INTO LEFTOVER SPACE between kitchen cabinets and a jog in the wall, this built-in desk is in a handy location, yet out of the way. Cabinets and open display shelves above the desk literally wrap around a small window that provides light and a nice view.

▲ HOUSED IN ITS OWN SMALL ALCOVE, this home work area has it all: a sense of privacy and a lovely view through its floor-to-ceiling windows. The thick glass desk surface is supported by built-in shelves and cabinets on both sides.

Utility Areas

THE LOWLY BUILT-IN CABINETS FOUND IN A UTILITY ROOM may not have the visual impact of fancy wall units found in more public areas of a home. However, they're a vital part of making the space useful for doing laundry and handling daily cleaning tasks. Raised counters provide space for sorting, folding, and stacking laundry. Sink cabinets support the fixtures and plumbing necessary for assorted clothes washing and cleaning duties. Shelves and storage cabinets provide a place to keep detergents and cleaning supplies out of sight. With the addition of child-proof locks, enclosed cabinets serve an even more vital purpose—keeping kids away from harmful chemicals.

If your utility area is in a space-challenged location, built-ins allow you to get the most from the space. For example, you can gain valuable storage by adding cabinetry or shelving above the washer/dryer. If you're fortunate enough to have a spacious utility room, you may want to outfit it with cabinetry that supports multiple functions, like shelving for old files. If it has an exterior entrance, your utility area also can serve as a mudroom with the addition of a coat rack, bench seat, and bins for shoe storage.

◀ A WELL-ORGANIZED UTILITY AREA is easy to work in and keep clean. The built-in cubbies here provide a place to keep towels, linens, and household supplies neatly arranged and stored. A countertop that runs above the washer and dryer creates a handy surface for clothes sorting.

◄ A TERRIFIC USE FOR BUILT-IN UTILITY ROOM CABINETRY is to hide unsightly things, such as waste cans, recycling bins, and water heaters. This cabinet has both a door and a hinged counter section that flips up to provide access to waste storage containers, as well as other stored items.

▼ THE MORE COUNTER SPACE YOU HAVE in your utility area the better. In this narrow space, counters run on either side. One caps the front-loading washer and dryer, while the other tops a lower cabinet that also houses a utility sink.

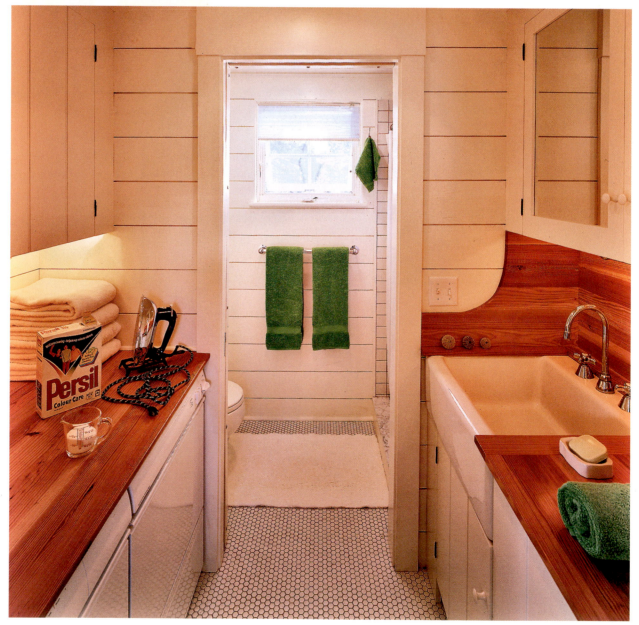

▲ IF YOUR HOME'S UTILITY ROOM has more space than you need for daily tasks, consider using the space to house other things. For example, mounting adjustable shelves on one or more walls can provide yards of storage for books, magazines, and more.

▲ YOU CAN USE UTILITY-AREA CABINETRY to do more than just house a washer and dryer. This room's built-ins include an upper supply storage cabinet, a set of bins for shoes, and a coat rack, all made from wood that matches the room's door and trim.

▲ **TO A GREAT EXTENT,** it's the cabinetry that puts the "utility" in a utility room. The built-in unit in this narrow space has a counter for groceries and parcels, drawers and doored storage compartments that hide clutter, and open cubbies that provide quick access to shoes, towels, and other items.

◄ EVEN A SMALL UTILITY ROOM can accommodate more than just a washer and dryer. This 80-sq.-ft. room features shoe storage cubbies beneath a laundry-folding counter, supply cabinets above the washer/dryer, and even a laundry shoot that delivers dirty clothes dropped from an upstairs bathroom.

▲ IN WET CLIMATES, a utility space can do double duty as a mudroom. This example has bench seating for donning and removing outdoor shoes, as well as cabinets and peg racks for hanging or storing clothes and sports equipment.

▼ ▶ **LOCATED BENEATH THE LAUNDRY CHUTE** in the utility room, this clever drawer can be loaded with clean towels and linens on the side shown in the photo at right. Here's the clever part: The drawer opens into an adjacent bathroom, where these clean items are readily accessed (shown in the photo below).

Resources

Taunton Press Publications

THE TAUNTON PRESS PUB-LISHES MANY OTHER TITLES IN THE IDEA BOOK SERIES ON TARGETED TOPICS OR PARTS OF THE HOME, IN-CLUDING:

Bouknight, Joanne Kellar. *Taunton's Home Storage Idea Book*. The Taunton Press, 2002.

Bouknight, Joanne Kellar. *Taunton's New Kitchen Idea Book*. The Taunton Press, 2004.

Jordan, Wendy. *New Kidspace Idea Book*. The Taunton Press, 2005.

Wormer, Andrew. *New Bathroom Idea Book*. The Taunton Press, 2004.

Zimmerman, Neal. *Home Workspace Idea Book*. The Taunton Press, 2002.

THE TAUNTON PRESS ALSO PUBLISHES THE FOLLOW-ING BOOKS ALL PACKED WITH PRACTICAL DESIGN IDEAS:

Susanka, Sarah. *The Not So Big House*. The Taunton Press, 1998.

Susanka, Sarah. *Creating the Not So Big House*. The Taunton Press, 2000.

Susanka, Sarah. *Not So Big Solutions for Your Home*. The Taunton Press, 2002.

Tolpin, Jim, with Mary Lathrop. *The New Family Home*. The Taunton Press, 2000.

Fine Homebuilding magazine is also a good resource; its special annual issues, *Houses* and *Kitchens and Baths*, are particularly useful.

Books

Carley, Rachel. *The Visual Dictionary of American Domestic Architecture*. Owl Books, 1997.

A useful illustrated reference that identifies and describes different styles of architecture (interiors and exteriors), from Federal style to the ranch house.

Hunter, Christine. *Ranches, Rowhouses & Railroad Flats*. WW Norton & Co, 1999.

A good read on the evolution of different forms of American housing, with an emphasis on environmental concerns.

Rybczynski, Witold. *Home: A Short History of an Idea*. Viking Penguin, 1986.

This book has become a classic, discussing the evolution of the idea of home, from medieval times to the present.

Websites

www.taunton.com/fhb

The website of Fine Homebuilding *magazine has links to a large list of information sites, manufacturers, and publications. Categories include environmentally conscious building, kit homes, kitchen and bath, and tools. This site is also a good source of product and design ideas, and has access to a forum for those interested in home design.*

www.build.com

This is a building and home improvement directory that provides links to manufacturers of building products, home products, building publications, and an extensive list of builders, designers, real estate agents, and mortgage brokers.

Professional Organizations

American Institute of Architects (AIA)
1735 New York Ave. NW
Washington, DC 20006
www.aiaaccess.com

Lists architects who are members of AIA. The website allows you to search for AIA architects in your area.

American Society of Interior Designers (ASID)
608 Massachusetts Ave. NE
Washington, DC 20002
Main website: www.asid.org
site: www.interiors.org

For names of ASID members in your area, go to the referral web

American Society of Landscape Architects (ASLA)
636 Eye St. NW
Washington, DC 20001
(202) 546-3480
www.asla.org.

Website offers tips on choosing a landscape architect and access to members.

Associated Landscape Contractors of America (ALCA)
150 Elden St., Suite 270
Herndon, VA 20170
(800) 395-ALCA
www.alca.org

Members are a mix of design/build contractors, installation, landscape maintenance, and interior landscape firms.

National Association of Home-Builders (NAHB)
1201 Fifteenth St. NW
Washington, DC 20005
(800) 368-5242
www.nahb.org

Includes builders and remodelers. website features consumer pages on planning a remodeling project and choosing a contractor.

National Association of the Remodeling Industry (NARI)
4900 Seminary Rd., #3210
Alexandria, VA 22311
(800) 611-6274
www.nari.org

This website provides a list of contractors.

National Kitchen & Bath Association
687 Willow Grove St.
Hackettstown, NJ 07840
www.nkba.com

Members are kitchen and bath design specialists. The website has projects, remodeling tips, and it lists design guidelines.

Credits

p. i: Photo: © Brian Vanden Brink, Photographer 2004.

p. iii: Photo: © Brian Vanden Brink, Photographer 2004.

p. iv: Photos (from left to right): © Brian Vanden Brink, Photographer 2004; © Robert Perron, Photographer; © Carolyn L. Bates–carolynbates.com.; © Brian Vanden Brink, Photographer 2004; © Carolyn L. Bates– carolynbates.com.

p. 1: All photos: © Brian Vanden Brink, Photographer 2004.

p. 2: (top) Photo: © Phillip Ennis Photography; (bottom) © Brian Vanden Brink, Photographer 2004.

p. 3: Photo: © Phillip Ennis Photography.

CHAPTER 1

p. 4: Photo: © Brian Vanden Brink, Photographer 2004.

p. 7: Photo: © Brian Vanden Brink, Photographer 2004.

p. 8: Photos: © www.davidduncanlivingston.com.

p. 9: Photos: © Brian Vanden Brink, Photographer 2004.

p. 10: Photo: © Carolyn L. Bates–carolynbates.com.

p. 11: Photos: © Brian Vanden Brink, Photographer 2004.

p. 12: Photo: © Carolyn L. Bates–carolynbates.com.

p. 13: Photos: © www.davidduncanlivingston.com.

CHAPTER 2

p. 14: Photo: © Robert Perron, Photographer.

p. 16: (left) Photo: © Brian Vanden Brink, Photographer 2004; (right) Photo: © Phillip Ennis Photography.

p. 17: Photo: © Brian Vanden Brink, Photographer 2004.

p. 18: Photo: © Phillip Ennis Photography.

p. 19: (left) Photo: © Brian Vanden Brink, Photographer 2004 (right) Photo: © Phillip Ennis Photography.

p. 20: Photos: © Brian Vanden Brink, Photographer 2004.

p. 21: Photo: © Carolyn L. Bates–carolynbates.com.

p. 22: Photos: © Brian Vanden Brink, Photographer 2004.

p. 23: (top) Photo: © www.davidduncanlivingston.com. (bottom) Photo: © Robert Perron, Photographer.

p. 24: (left) Photo: © Brian Vanden Brink, Photographer 2004; (right) Photo: © www.davidduncanlivingston.com.

p. 25: Photo: © Phillip Ennis Photography.

p. 26: (top left) Photo: © Brian Vanden Brink, Photographer 2004; (top right) Photo: © www.davidduncanlivingston.com; (bottom) Photo: © Carolyn L. Bates–carolynbates.com.

p. 27: Photo: © Brian Vanden Brink, Photographer 2004.

CHAPTER 3

p. 28: Photo: © Carolyn L. Bates–carolynbates.com.

p. 30: (top)Photo: © Phillip Ennis Photography; (botom) Photo: © Carolyn L. Bates–carolynbates.com.

p. 31: Photos: © Ken Gutmaker.

p. 32: Photo: © Carolyn L. Bates–carolynbates.com.

p. 33: Photo: © Brian Vanden Brink, Photographer 2004.

p. 34: (top) Photo: © Carolyn L. Bates–carolynbates.com; (bottom) Photo: © Brian Vanden Brink, Photographer 2004.

p. 35: (top) Photo: © Mark Samu; (bottom) Photo: © Chipper Hatter.

p. 36: Photos: © Phillip Ennis Photography.

p. 37: (left) Photo: © Chipper Hatter; (right) Photo: © Mark Samu.

p. 38: (left) Photo: © Brian Vanden Brink, Photographer 2004; (top right) Photo: © www.davidduncanlivingston.com; (bottom right) Photo: © Phillip Ennis Photography.

p. 39: Photo: © Brian Vanden Brink, Photographer 2004.

p. 40: (left) Photo: © Phillip Ennis Photography; (right) Photo: © Brian Vanden Brink, Photographer 2004.

p. 41: Photos: © Brian Vanden Brink, Photographer 2004.

p. 42: Photo: © Mark Samu.

p. 43: (top)Photo: © www.davidduncanlivingston.com; (bottom left)Photo: © Brian Vanden Brink, Photographer 2004; (bottom right) Photo: © Brian Vanden Brink, Photographer 2004.

p. 44: (left) Photo: © Mark Samu; (right) Photo: © Chipper Hatter.

p. 45: (top) Photo: © Phillip Ennis Photography; (bottom) Photo: © Carolyn L. Bates–carolynbates.com.

p. 46: (left) Photo: © Mark Samu; (right) Photo: © Andrew Wormer.

p. 47: Photos: © Mark Samu.

p. 48: (bottom left) Photo:© Mark Samu; (top right) Photo: © Brian Vanden Brink, Photographer 2004.

p. 49: Photos: © Phillip Ennis Photography.

p. 50: (top) Photo: © Brian Vanden Brink, Photographer 2004; (bottom) Photo: © Phillip Ennis Photography.

p. 51: (top) Photo: © Phillip Ennis Photography; (bottom) Photo: © Mark Samu.

p. 52: Photo: © Carolyn L. Bates–carolynbates.com.

p. 53: (left) Photo: © Mark Samu; (right) Photo: © Carolyn L. Bates–carolynbates.com.

p. 54: Photos: © Phillip Ennis Photography.

p. 55: Photo: © Brian Vanden Brink, Photographer 2004.

p. 56: Photo: © Carolyn L. Bates–carolynbates.com.

p. 57: (top) Photo: © Carolyn L. Bates–carolynbates.com; (bottom) Photo: © Phillip Ennis Photography.

p. 58 & 59: Photos: © Brian Vanden Brink, Photographer 2004.

p. 60: (top) Photo: © Brian Vanden Brink, Photographer 2004; (bottom) Photo: © Phillip Ennis Photography.

p. 61: (left) Photo: © Chipper Hatter; (right) Photo: © Robert Perron, Photographer.

p. 62: (top) Photo: © Double D Photoworks; (bottom) Photo: Roe Osborn, courtesy *Fine Homebuilding*, © The Taunton Press, Inc.

p. 63: (top) Photo: Charles Miller, courtesy *Fine Homebuilding*, © The Taunton Press, Inc.; (bottom) Photo: Roe Osborn, courtesy *Fine Homebuilding*, © The Taunton Press, Inc.

p. 64: Photos: © Brian Vanden Brink, Photographer 2004.

p. 65: Photo: © Mark Samu.

CHAPTER 4

p. 66 & 67: Photos: © Brian Vanden Brink, Photographer 2004.

p. 68: Photo: © Norman McGrath.

p. 69: (left) Photo: © Mark Samu; (right) Photo: © Phillip Ennis Photography.

p. 70: (top) Photo: © Phillip Ennis Photography; (bottom) Photo: © Carolyn L. Bates–carolynbates.com.

p. 71: Photos: © Brian Vanden Brink, Photographer 2004.

p. 72: (left) Photo: © Randi Baird; (right) Photo: Charles Miller, courtesy *Fine Homebuilding*, © The Taunton Press, Inc.

p. 73: Photo: © Chipper Hatter.

p. 74: (top) Photo: © Carolyn L. Bates–carolynbates.com; (bottom) Photo: © Chipper Hatter.

p. 75: (top) Photo: © Carolyn L. Bates–carolynbates.com; (center and bottom) Photos: © Mark Samu.

p. 76: (top) Photo: © Brian Vanden Brink, Photographer 2004; (bottom) Photo: © Carolyn L. Bates–carolynbates.com.

p. 77: Photo: Andy Engel, courtesy *Fine Homebuilding*, © The Taunton Press, Inc.

CHAPTER 5

p. 78: Photo: © Brian Vanden Brink, Photographer 2004.

p. 79–83: Photos: © Brian Vanden Brink, Photographer 2004.

p. 84: Photos: © Carolyn L. Bates–carolynbates.com.

p. 85: (top) Photo: © Robert Perron, Photographer; (bottom) Photo: © Brian Vanden Brink, Photographer 2004.

p. 86: Photo: © Carolyn L. Bates–carolynbates.com.

p. 87: (top) Photo: © Phillip Ennis Photography; (bottom) Photo: © Brian Vanden Brink, Photographer 2004.

p. 88: (top) Photo: © Chipper Hatter; (bottom) Photo: © Brian Vanden Brink, Photographer 2004.

p. 89: (top) Photo: © Brian Vanden Brink, Photographer 2004; (bottom left) Photo: © Carolyn L. Bates–carolynbates.com; (bottom right) Photo: © Mark Samu.

p. 90: (top) Photo: © Chipper Hatter; (bottom) Photo: © Carolyn L. Bates–carolynbates.com.

p. 91: (top) Photo: © Phillip Ennis Photography; (bottom) Photo: © Carolyn L. Bates–carolynbates.com.

p. 92: Photo: © Brian Vanden Brink, Photographer 2004.

p. 93: (top) Photo: © Brian Vanden Brink, Photographer 2004; (bottom) Photo: © Phillip Ennis Photography.

p. 94: Photo: © Carolyn L. Bates–carolynbates.com.

p. 95: (top) Photo: © Carolyn L. Bates–carolynbates.com; (bottom) Photo: © Phillip Ennis Photography.

p. 96: (top) Photo: © Robert Perron, Photographer; (bottom) Photo: © Brian Vanden Brink, Photographer 2004.

p. 97: (top) Photo: © www.davidduncanlivingston.com; (bottom) Photo: © Mark Samu.

p. 98: (top) Photo: © Carolyn L. Bates– carolynbates.com; (bottom) Photo: © Phillip Ennis Photography.
p. 99: (top) Photo: © Robert Perron, Photographer; (bottom) Photo: © Phillip Ennis Photography.

CHAPTER 6

p. 100 & 102: Photo: © Brian Vanden Brink, Photographer 2004.
p. 103: Photos: © Harriet Robinson/Dave Adamson, Lone Pine Pictures.
p. 104: (top) Photo: © www.davidduncanlivingston.com; (bottom) Photo: © Robert Perron, Photographer.
p. 105 & 106: Photos: © Phillip Ennis Photography.
p. 107: Photos: © John Marckworth.
p. 108: (top left) Photo: © Brian Vanden Brink, Photographer 2004; (top right & bottom) Photo: © Phillip Ennis Photography.
p. 109: Photo: © Brian Vanden Brink, Photographer 2004.
p. 110: Photo: © Phillip Ennis Photography.
p. 111: (top) Photo: © Robert Perron, Photographer; (bottom) Photo: © www.davidduncanlivingston.com.
p. 112: (top) Photo: © Brian Vanden Brink, Photographer 2004; (bottom) Photo:© Carolyn L. Bates-www.carolynbates.com.
p. 113: (top) Photo: Scott Gibson, courtesy *Fine Homebuilding,* © The Taunton Press, Inc.; (bottom) Photo: Charles Miller, courtesy *Fine Homebuilding,* © The Taunton Press, Inc.

CHAPTER 7

p. 114:Photo: © Brian Vanden Brink, Photographer 2004.
p. 116: Photo: © Mark Samu.
p. 117: Photos: © Phillip Ennis Photography.
p. 118: Photos: © Norman McGrath.
p. 119: (top) Photo: © Robert Perron, Photographer; (bottom) Photo: © Brian Vanden Brink, Photographer 2004.
p. 120: (top left) Photo: © Carolyn L. Bates–carolynbates.com; (bottom left) Photo: © Brian Vanden Brink, Photographer 2004; (right) Photo: © www.davidduncanlivingston.com.
p. 121: (top) Photo: © Carolyn L. Bates– carolynbates.com; (bottom) Photo: © Brian Vanden Brink, Photographer 2004.
p. 122: Photo: © Phillip Ennis Photography.

p. 123: (top) Photo: © Phillip Ennis Photography; (center & bottom) Photo: © Brian Vanden Brink, Photographer 2004.
p. 124: (top) Photo: © Carolyn L. Bates–carolynbates.com; (bottom) Photo: © Brian Vanden Brink, Photographer 2004.
p. 125: Photo: © Mark Samu.
p. 126: Photo: © Brian Vanden Brink, Photographer 2004.
p. 127: (top) Photos: © Norman McGrath; (bottom) Photo: © Brian Vanden Brink, Photographer 2004.
p. 128: Photo: © Brian Vanden Brink, Photographer 2004.
p. 129: (left) Photo: © Carolyn L. Bates–carolynbates.com; (right) Photo: © Phillip Ennis Photography.
p. 130: (left) Photo: © Brian Vanden Brink, Photographer 2004; (right) Photo: © Phillip Ennis Photography.
p. 131: Photo: © Phillip Ennis Photography.

CHAPTER 8

p. 132: Photo: © Brian Vanden Brink, Photographer 2004.
p. 134: Photos: © www.davidduncanlivingston.com.
p. 135: Photo: © Mark Samu.
p. 136: Photo: © Phillip Ennis Photography.
p. 137: (top) Photo: © Carolyn L. Bates–carolynbates.com; (right) Photo: © Mark Samu.
p. 138: (top) Photo: Roe Osborn, courtesy *Fine Homebuilding,* © The Taunton Press, Inc.; (bottom) Photo: © www.davidduncanlivingston.com.
p. 139: Photo: © www.davidduncanlivingston.com.
p. 140: (top) Photo: © Norman McGrath; (bottom) Photo: © Mark Samu.
p. 141: Photo: © www.davidduncanlivingston.com.
p. 142: Photo: © Mark Samu.
p. 143: (top) Photo: © Phillip Ennis Photography; (bottom) Photo: © Tim Ebert

CHAPTER 9

p. 144: Photo: © Brian Vanden Brink, Photographer 2004.
p. 145 & 146: Photo: © Mark Samu.
p. 147: Photos: © Brian Vanden Brink, Photographer 2004.
p. 148: Photo: © Norman McGrath.
p. 149: (top) Photo: © Norman McGrath; (bottom) Photo: © Ken Gutmaker.

p. 150: (top) © ww.davidduncanlivingston.com; (bottom) Photo: © Carolyn L. bates–carolynbates.com.
p. 151: Photo: © Phillip Ennis Photography.
p. 152: (top) Photo: © Brian Vanden Brink, Photographer 2004; (bottom) Photo: Roe Osborn, courtesy *Fine Homebuilding,* © The Taunton Press, Inc.
p. 153: Photo: © Carolyn L. Bates– carolynbates.com.
p. 154 & 155: Photos:© www.davidduncanlivingston.com.
p. 156: (top) Photo: © Carolyn L. Bates–carolynbates.com; (bottom) Photo: © Phillip Ennis Photography.
p. 157: Photo: © www.davidduncanlivingston.com.
p. 158: (top) Photo: © Mark Samu; (bottom) Photo: © Phillip Ennis Photography.
p. 159:(top) Photo: © www.davidduncanlivingston.com; (bottom) Photo: © Carolyn L. Bates–carolynbates.com.
p. 160: (top) Photo: © Mark Samu; (bottom) Photo: © Phillip Ennis Photography.
p. 161: Photos: Charles Miller, courtesy *Fine Homebuilding,* © The Taunton Press, Inc.

CHAPTER 10

p. 162: Photo: © Brian Vanden Brink, Photographer 2004.
p. 163: Photo: © Robert Perron, Photographer.
p. 164: (top) Photo: © Mark Samu; (bottom) Photo: © Brian Vanden Brink, Photographer 2004.
p. 165: Photo: © www.davidduncanlivingston.com.
p. 166: Photo: © Randy O'Rourke.
p. 167: (top) Photo: Andy Engel, courtesy *Fine Homebuilding,* © The Taunton Press, Inc.; (bottom) Photo: © Robert Benson Photography.
p. 168: Photos: Andy Engel, courtesy *Fine Homebuilding,* © The Taunton Press, Inc.

For More Great Design Ideas, Look for These and Other Taunton Press Books wherever Books are Sold.

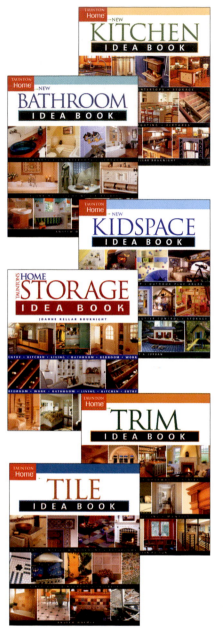

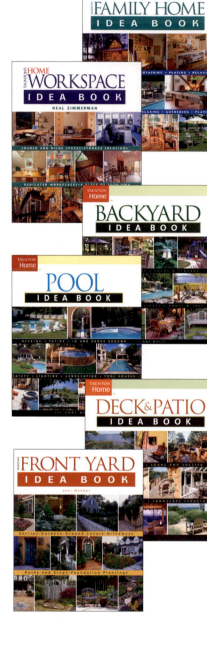

NEW KITCHEN IDEA BOOK
ISBN 1-56158-693-5
Product #070773
$19.95 U.S.
$27.95 Canada

NEW BATHROOM IDEA BOOK
ISBN 1-56158-692-7
Product #070774
$19.95 U.S.
$27.95 Canada

NEW KIDSPACE IDEA BOOK
ISBN 1-56158-694-3
Product #070776
$19.95 U.S.
$27.95 Canada

TAUNTON'S HOME STORAGE IDEA BOOK
ISBN 1-56158-676-5
Product #070758
$19.95 U.S.
$27.95 Canada

TRIM IDEA BOOK
ISBN 1-56158-710-9
Product #070786
$19.95 U.S.
$27.95 Canada

TILE IDEA BOOK
ISBN 1-56158-709-5
Product #07075
$19.95 U.S.
$27.95 Canada

TAUNTON'S FAMILY HOME IDEA BOOK
ISBN 1-56158-729-X
Product #070789
$19.95 U.S.
$27.95 Canada

TAUNTON'S HOME WORKSPACE IDEA BOOK
ISBN 1-56158-701-X
Product #070783
$19.95 U.S.
$27.95 Canada

BACKYARD IDEA BOOK
ISBN 1-56158-667-6
Product #070749
$19.95 U.S.
$27.95 Canada

POOL IDEA BOOK
ISBN 1-56158-764-8
Product #070825
$19.95 U.S.
$27.95 Canada

DECK & PATIO IDEA BOOK
ISBN 1-56158-639-0
Product #070718
$19.95 U.S.
$27.95 Canada

TAUNTON'S FRONT YARD IDEA BOOK
ISBN 1-56158-519-X
Product #070621
$19.95 U.S.
$27.95 Canada